HOW TO BE HAPPY BEING YOU

HOW TO BE HAPPY BEING YOU

DENNIS M. HARGIS

Anamcara Press LLC

Published in 2024 by Anamcara Press LLC
Author © 2024 by Dennis M. Hargis
Cover art and design by Julia Cubiz, Outcasted Art
Book design by Maureen Carroll
Arial, Tomarik, Lato, Professor Minty
Printed in the United States of America.

Book description: Psychologist Dennis Hargis's unique and successful program is designed to help young people explore feelings and apply problem-solving techniques to tough emotional issues faced by adolescents.

All rights reserved. No part of this publication may be reproduced, distributed, or transmitted in any form or by any means, including photocopying, recording, or other electronic or mechanical methods, without the prior written permission of the publisher, except in the case of brief quotations embodied in critical reviews and certain other noncommercial uses permitted by copyright law. For permission requests, write to the publisher, addressed "Attention: Permissions Coordinator," at the address below.

ANAMCARA PRESS LLC
P.O. Box 442072, Lawrence, KS 66044
https://anamcara-press.com

Ordering Information:
Quantity sales. Special discounts are available on quantity purchases by corporations, associations, and others. For details, contact the publisher at the address above. Orders by U.S. trade bookstores and wholesalers. Please contact Ingram Distribution.

ISBN-13: How to be Happy Being You, 978-1-960462-06-0 (Paperback)
ISBN-13: How to be Happy Being You, 978-1-960462-07-7 (EBook)
ISBN-13: How to be Happy Being You, 978-1-960462-08-4 (Hardcover)
YAN051060 / YOUNG ADULT NONFICTION / Social Topics / Depression & Mental Illness
YAN024100 YOUNG ADULT NONFICTION / Health & Daily Living / Mental Health
YAN048040 YOUNG ADULT NONFICTION / Religious / Christian / Inspirational
YAN024050 YOUNG ADULT NONFICTION / Health & Daily Living / Maturing

Library of Congress Control Number: 2023939071

To my sons Bobby, Tommy, and Michael;
in memory of my parents Ernestine and Harry Hargis;
and to my cousin (best friend) Ronnie.

CONTENTS

Chapter 1: Who, Why And How 1
Chapter 2: Special Challenges—Is This You? 7
Chapter 3: Anger 12
Chapter 4: The World of Feelings and How We Deal with Them .. 70
Chapter 5: It's All About Character! 146
Chapter 6: Everyday Miracles 199
Chapter 7: The World Needs You! 202
Appendix A 207
Appendix B 209
Appendix C 213
Acknowledgements 219
About the Author 221
About the Artist 223

A Special Note to Readers:

This book is intended for any young person who wants to be happier and learn how to handle life's challenges, but if you have a more serious issue, you need this book even more.

If you are thinking of suicide or committing an act of violence to inflict pain on others, please do NOT do anything until you give yourself a chance by reading this book. Both acts are often seen as desperate pleas to be noticed and remembered. There are far better ways to do that.

If you are thinking about suicide, it's probably because you are in a situation where you believe there is no way out, or you want to punish others by leaving them with guilt and blame. **First, time changes everything. Whatever your world is today, it can and will change.** If you are trying to make others feel guilty or sorry, you miss out on the opportunity to show them how valuable you really are in this world.

If you are thinking of doing harm with a violent or catastrophic act to get even or punish others and to make them sorry, you will suffer too—either the fate of your victim(s), or be doomed to live the rest of your days having a lowly and unimportant existence. If you think it is a way to be noticed, after a while, no one will remember your name, only the crime. Instead, people tend to remember the names of those who make the world a better place and are examples of goodness and service to others. We all want heroes, not villains.

If either of these situations describe what you are contemplating, let's find a better way together and make your life meaningful and happy.

Chapter 1: Who, Why And How

Who Should Read This Book

I wrote this book for **YOU** because now is probably a confusing stage in your life. You could be fourteen, maybe seventeen, or somewhere close in age. You have left your childhood behind and now are embarking on the most exciting or maybe challenging part of your life. For most, it is great to be in your teenage years, but for some, it could be a time of difficulty and trouble. In either case, you are an important part of the generation that will shape the world, although you may not realize this if your life seems to be a roller coaster of extreme emotions, both high and low, making you unhappy. If so, I want to help you change that.

School is a major focus for your age group where you make new friends, study academics and world events, participate in things that interest you, and where you can begin to identify your talents and gifts. But this stage in your development toward adulthood isn't free of challenges by any means. Establishing social relationships is one of them with dating beginning around the age of fifteen. Add to that, sexual urges which require you to learn "how to control yourself."

There are a number of factors that might have occurred in your past that will affect you now and in the future, especially your communication and interpersonal skills in developing relationships. Believe it or not, much of your current well-being is rooted in your childhood. If it was happy, you likely will not have many issues to resolve, but if you were a victim of abuse or neglect, that could and probably will, affect your relationships, your health, and your mental outlook, but there are ways to lessen the impact.

If abuse happened in your childhood, it is critical to identify and confront those deep-seated feelings, as difficult as it is, and some may even be buried deep into your subconscious mind. Feelings of shame and guilt are two of the culprits that often result and can distort your view of the world to make it difficult to communicate and form relationships. That's why it's important to identify these painful feelings and the events that led to them.

Divorce of your parents is another occurrence that might have affected you. It is an unstable time in a family's life where pain and anger are rampant, and can be felt years after. Children often internalize the blame for their parents' separation, feeling that it is their fault. This may lead to mixed-up feelings in adulthood and create problems, some you may not even realize. This makes it even more important to understand how our feelings work inside our bodies. Getting in touch with your feelings, developing problem-solving skills, using consultation and collaboration when working on projects with groups of people, and incorporating virtues (what I consider to be character coping skills) into your daily life are the challenges you face.

Even if you haven't experienced trauma in childhood, you may still have a lot of anxiety. That's normal, especially because you are exposed to many new situations, people and feelings. We adults have left you with quite a mess to clean up. There are wars and tension between nations, and even among people in our country. Mass shootings are increasing at an alarming rate. Crime is on the rise, ravishing our cities. Racism runs deep. Climate change threatens the destruction of our planet and more animals are becoming extinct. A growing number of people are starving and homeless. And this isn't just in the United States; it's a scary time in history for the whole world. Because there is so much stress and worry, anger is also rampant and drives so much of our reaction to what happens in our lives, and that is why this book devotes a great deal of content to it to help you understand and respond in a way that is best for you and for others.

I was raised in a loving home with parents who valued the moral development of their children. They taught us to have respect, kindness, and courtesy for others. Perhaps religion has not been a factor for you, but the spiritual dimension of life is so important that it can't be discarded. Even if you didn't have the type of childhood I had, please give the program included in this book a chance and, I truly believe, you *do* have the power to make a difference, and to be happy!

Why This Book Can Help You

I STARTED WORKING WITH CHILDREN AND YOUTH, beginning at the age of 15 as a summer school counselor. While in college, I worked as an assistant teacher at a day care for exceptional children. Upon graduating, I served four school districts as a school psychologist that included elementary, middle, and high school students. During that time, I created several special education programs for students with learning disabilities and those with behavioral disorders. My career then evolved into quite a unique job. I became the school psychologist at Osawatomie State Hospital in Kansas and, eventually, the principal of the school which was located on the hospital grounds to serve adolescents with severe emotional and mental health issues. There was also a Youth Center for troubled adolescents, those who had committed criminal infractions. We provided educational services to them as well.

There, I also developed an anger management program for youth. My job then led to the role of a crisis intervention specialist. Whenever a patient was out of control in a classroom, I would be called in to help defuse the situation. My job was to keep everyone safe and prevent patients from hurting teachers, other students, and even themselves. The job was dangerous at times because I had to restrain students, break up fights, and take sharp objects away. Yet in 16 years of service, I was never hurt and I never received one single complaint from a patient or student. How was that possible? Welcome to the power of character coping skills or what I call "virtues." I loved the patients and they knew it. I <u>respected</u> and <u>accepted</u> them for who they were and they knew it. I showed <u>kindness</u> and <u>compassion</u> to them daily and they felt it. These virtues allowed us to establish a friendship. Even when they were out of control, they never hurt me because we had a special bond.

Later, I became a principal for a special purpose school before ending my career again as an elementary school principal. During my more than 40 years of working with children and youth, I have gained insight to help you in the difficult challenges that you have to face in today's world. In this book, I can help you to acquire the virtues to make a difference too.

How To Use This Book

THIS BOOK IS SPECIFICALLY FOR **YOU**—AN adolescent/teenager/young adult—to empower and give you resources that will reduce the anxiety or pain in your life so you can be happier and more productive in your world. It is filled with practical assistance, and consists of activities and exercises that have been successfully used many times. It can also be a great resource to use for on-the-spot conflicts. This book is easy to comprehend, and illustrations are plentiful to help you understand the information. You will be able to use the book immediately to help with your problem-solving and communication skills, both critical in helping you navigate your place in the world.

To get the full benefit of the information imparted in this book, it is preferable for you to read every page and complete every exercise. You can benefit from the exercises by answering the questions mentally or by writing your responses in a separate note pad. Later, you can search by feelings, or even situations to learn the best way to handle them, but first, I will help you to identify your true feelings. That is important because sometimes the cause for a particular feeling like depression or sadness can be hidden, even from your conscious mind. Once known, you can determine the best way to confront the cause and express yourself to ease your pain or anger.

You may occasionally even notice some duplication of information across the various sections. That is because it is pertinent to more than one subject, or its importance bears repeating. When referencing individual parts of the book over time, these repetitions are especially crucial for understanding the information.

Finally, it's helpful to note that this book uses seven basic steps:

1. **Explore the nature of anger**
2. **Identify your behavior in anger-provoking situations**
3. **Channel your anger with specific techniques**
4. **Identify your painful and undesirable feelings**
5. **Learn to problem-solve**
6. **Strengthen your virtues**
7. **Practice. Practice. Practice**

More than ever, we need a renewed spirituality of unity in a world where justice is the guiding factor, and love and respect for our fellow man is the guiding force. It is *you* and your generation who will become the leaders in this quest. To do this, you need to be empowered, to be happy with yourself, and find your unique place in the world. Let's work on this together.

Chapter 2: Special Challenges— Is This You?

It's Normal

You are not alone! Don't think, for a moment, that you are the only one who has disturbing thoughts and painful feelings. You may feel powerless, overwhelmed, or maybe even hopeless. It's okay. We all occasionally have these thoughts, these feelings. If only we could remember at the time that our thoughts and feelings are just temporary, and that we have the power to make them so. Often, we forget that fact because of our emotional state.

When negative thoughts and feelings go past a week or two, talking to a friend, your parents, a teacher, a counselor, or a school social worker is the preferred course of action. Bottling up and ignoring feelings is the *wrong* thing to do. If the problem goes beyond several weeks, you might need to consult someone trained in mental health. There is no shame in asking for help. We all need support. While it's normal to be unhappy sometimes, it's not normal to be unhappy all or most of the time. This is when thoughts of harming yourself or others might occur. **Please don't be discouraged and find a solution by yourself that will be a permanent one to a temporary problem!**

Even if you are enjoying your life, it does and will have its pitfalls. You have to keep up with your academics, develop social skills, establish relationships with your friends, and for some, tolerate your parents. Communication plays an important role in all of these. Knowing yourself, and recognizing personal issues that affect how and what you do, is vital when it comes to associating with others. You may have bad things happen like a death in the family or your parents decide to divorce, or you are poor and lack in sufficient food and clothing. These are all troubling events when any of us could have a moment where we let our feelings take control of us. You are no different. Life is a test of mastering the difficulties we encounter daily, but your childhood and past experiences also influence how you see the world today.

Special Education/Disability

LOOKING BACK, IF YOU ARE A STUDENT who received special education services, or are physically handicapped, your early road in school was or still is different from the other students. You may have struggled with your reading skills which lagged far behind your classmates. You might have had difficulty with math or writing. Those of you with physical handicaps could have had difficulty with mobility, just getting around school or, perhaps, it was more serious. The bottom line—you had to overcome hardships, and maybe even bullying that the average students were free from. Professionals often refer to students who are behind in academics as being "learning disabled." What does this mean? If you are a student with this label, you may actually possess average or above average intelligence in comparison to the other students, but the learning style (unique to you) was different and not taught in the regular education curriculum. You might have thought, and still do, you were just dumb. This might have affected your self-esteem and your ability to fully explore and find your special place in the world.

If you're a teenager assigned to a mental facility or have been in intense therapy, it's likely you come from a dysfunctional family. In these cases, the first thing the staff or therapist will probably do is to try to find the right medications to help you control your behavior. One of the problems that teenagers (and even adults) sometimes have in this situation is that they get on the right medicines, improve their coping behaviors, and after release, fail to continue to take the medication prescribed. Then as no surprise, they begin having the same problems if the underlying cause of the anger and the feeling itself aren't acknowledged and addressed. This is not easy, by any means, but that is the challenge.

Confined Facilities

WHAT ABOUT THOSE OF YOU WHO FIND yourself confined to youth centers or have been in the past? Not surprisingly, any type of correctional facility creates a real challenge. Once away from that environment, you are going to have to put out a great deal of effort for self-improvement. Maybe before, you fell into the company of negative influences. It doesn't matter now. You can control your future. You are still young and capable of making the changes to turn your life around.

You may encounter people who might refer to you as a juvenile delinquent. They have already passed judgment on you, labeled you, and want you to stay away from their families. How does it feel to be isolated, to be disliked by so many people? Are they even going to give you a chance to learn new skills and improve your behavior, or are they going to stay entrenched in their prejudiced beliefs about you? I imagine that there will be some who are going to retain their prejudice, and then there are some who are willing to open their hearts and give you another chance. No matter how others see you, the most important factor here is knowing yourself—being aware of your feelings, being able to effectively problem-solve, discover how to improve your communication skills, and then acquire virtues or character coping skills mentioned earlier. No matter what you think, virtues really are important, and with them, the future can still be bright. Make sure it's positive and beneficial for **you**.

LGBTQ

IF YOU ARE LESBIAN, GAY, BISEXUAL, OR transgender, you have a very difficult road to travel. Frequently, you may be ostracized by others in and out of school, or the target of ridicule and bullies. Even in your family your mom, dad, or other family members and relatives may refuse to accept you for the person you are. Hopefully, you are one of the lucky ones who have supportive parents. Society, for the most part, is critical of your orientation. Things are getting better, but here is the scary news. Research tells us you are 6 times more likely to experience symptoms of depression, and 3 ½ times more likely to attempt suicide than others in your age group. So, what can you do? Find a support group of peers your own age, friends. Talk to them. Share your anxieties and your feelings. Look for a caring and empathetic adult, or maybe two, that you can trust and confide in. This person could be a teacher, a school counselor, an understanding parent, or a mental health professional. Whatever you do, don't isolate yourself. You, more than anyone else, need to be in touch with your feelings so you can be on guard from outside negative impact.

Change Is Up To YOU

WHETHER OR NOT YOU CAN IDENTIFY WITH any of the special challenges in this chapter, enriching relationships, even if you don't think so, is a goal everyone wants to achieve. By gathering the right information, you can get in touch with your emotional-self and become aware of your intellectual-self to help you handle difficult situations. You can make changes in your life so it is more fulfilling and meaningful, but only you may choose this path. People don't change out of force or fear. They might change in the short term, but nothing lasting over time. To make a permanent change, you must consciously want to change. Once decided, insight must occur first before the change is possible, otherwise, you will reuse the same ineffective skills over and over. Insight must come from you, not from the beliefs of others who may try to convince you of the errors of your ways. People change when they become aware of the need to change. People change when they have the desire to change. No one can help you if you don't want to be helped. No one else can make you have lasting change, but be proud of yourself when you engage in positive behavior to make progress toward a better you.

Chapter 3: Anger

Where Anger Comes From

Anger is rampant and drives much of our reaction to what happens in our lives, making it imperative to understand and respond to it in a way that is best for you and for others. But where does anger come from? Surprisingly, many people can't answer this simple question.

Anger comes from the thoughts we form in our mind. To be more specific, it is the way we interpret events that happen in our life that leads to our anger. It can take the form of mild irritation to intense rage. For example, someone at the restaurant bumps into you and spills a drink all over your new clothes. You're a new student at a local high school and someone trips you while you are walking down the hallway. You are driving along and someone cuts in front of you, nearly hitting your car. If you interpret these events as an accident, you might dismiss the incidents as unfortunate, but no big deal. If you think the action was deliberate, you believe that an injustice was committed against you and you become upset. You may even want to get some degree of revenge. What might make one person angry may have little or no effect on someone else.

Anger is a very powerful emotion. Because our thoughts, as we interpret them, are the source of our anger along with other feelings that determine our actions, anger can break up families, lead to possible alcohol and drug addiction, make us susceptible to medical problems, destroy our relationships with others, and lead to confinement in jail or prison. However, there is a positive side to anger. You can also use it to improve yourself, study harder, exercise more, and work toward charitable enterprises to achieve your goals. How you deal with anger can make you or break you. In fact, how you deal with it may be a better determiner of success than intelligence.

We have a myth in our society that if you have an anger problem or you have to cope with a painful feeling, then there is something inherently wrong with you. This makes many people afraid to seek help. They don't want to be labeled as bad, evil, weak or worthless which can attack the core of their self-esteem. By understanding how anger works and providing management techniques to use, undesirable feelings and combative, resistive and defensive behavior can be reduced.

Factors That Influence The Way We Express Our Anger

HOW WE EXPRESS OUR ANGER IS A *LEARNED BEHAVIOR*. You learn about anger from your own personal experiences with the world while growing up: families, friends, neighborhood, school, church, television, movies, video games—everything that surrounds you. Of course, parents are the predominant role models. If your parents yell at each other or at you and your siblings, you and they will tend to yell at each other and other people.

Some parents teach their kids to ignore their anger and are encouraged to refrain from expressing it, to "hold it in." Unfortunately, this practice also has an unhealthy effect. Anger that is suppressed over an extended period of time can lead to depression, unhappiness, and less stability. Then there are some parents who are violent role models. Their children are exposed to yelling and hitting, and then coaxed to hit their peers and stop "being a baby." Both the "holding in" reaction to anger, and the hitting or "letting it out" are unhealthy ways to teach anger management to impressionable children. These may lead to life-long problems such as bullying or withdrawn personalities.

How your parents disciplined you is very important in how you channel your feelings now and in the future, especially anger. Awareness of these patterns is important because much effort will be required to overcome a learned expression of anger that is inappropriate.

A second factor in how we express anger originates from abuse which can occur in various ways—physical, emotional, sexual, neglect and abandonment. Because abuse can come from anyone and anywhere, the effects can be devastating to a child's development in learning to trust, not live in fear, communicate feelings, etc. Unfortunately, abuse occurs more often than we might think.

Physical abuse occurs when purposely inflicting pain to hurt a child's body, especially in cases of severe punishment. Then there is emotional abuse which could involve ridicule and constant yelling. Sexual abuse might entail touching in an inappropriate way or exposing a child to materials, through various media, beyond his or her maturational development. Neglect, another form of abuse, occurs if the child's physical, psychological, and emotional needs are ignored. These are just brief descriptions of abuse that affect children and can have lasting problems for them over their lifetimes.

Bullying and cyberbullying need to be added to the list of childhood trauma. Bullying can lead to both physical and emotional scars. You may have been a victim of this type of abuse or know of someone who has been. Most everyone who has been bullied can still remember those events and who did them, even well into adulthood. Perpetrators make life, at the time, miserable. Cyberbullying is just another form of bullying that occurs on social media, through emails, texts, chats, etc. In extreme cases, the ridicule can lead to suicide for the victims.

The painful feelings that are caused by these aforementioned environmental events, especially shame and guilt, may be "stored up" in the body and mind over time, and can later affect a person's interactions with peers and adults. They leave scars that must be recognized and addressed. A person trained in mental health assistance can often help. Important to note is that occasional negative events are radically different from experiencing abuse, neglect, or abandonment. These treacherous acts leave emotional scars on your soul. They attack the spirit and damage you, maybe throughout adulthood without some type of intervention. If you have an abundant share of these experiences, your mind and body will store them up, repress (bury) them, and keep you unaware of their effects on your present-day behavior.

Adults who have been abused and neglected as children may see the world as distorted, making them more susceptible to anger and other deep-seated painful feelings. Fortunately, people are resilient, and you can be too if you are or have been a victim of abuse. It may be hard to believe, but as time passes, wounds lessen in their intensity. Hope and better times light up the future, but you must first bring the negative feelings to a conscious level and find ways to cope with them (included in later chapters). However, as noted earlier, in severe cases, you may need the help of someone who is trained to help victims of abuse so that you gain insight into the pain you endured as a child. **Note: if you are still experiencing abuse, please don't wait. Tell a trusted adult, and keep doing so until you find someone to help.**

Genetics could be another contributing factor in how you express anger, but there is no valid research to support a hereditary link in family histories. The concept is that if you had a parent or other close relative like an aunt or uncle with an explosive anger problem, you might inherit their predisposition. Maybe your mother tells you that your cousin acts just like your grandpa Jeff on your father's side; that's where he gets his "hateful" personality. If this is the case, some people may have to work harder at controlling their emotions because they inherited a gene that triggers anger and aggression. More likely, the expression of anger is learned in families as explained previously.

Your *emotional state of mind,* when presented with a stressor (something known to cause you angst), has a large impact on your reaction. For example, a determiner of how you respond to a situation could be lack of sleep, worry about your mother who was just diagnosed with cancer, worry that your father and mother aren't getting along and considering a divorce, or fear about a big test coming up that could affect your GPA and scholarship opportunities. Each of these life events can place your emotional mind on edge. Even drugs like alcohol, nicotine, and caffeine produce irritability and unrest after their effects wear off. All of these situations may even cause you to say things that you don't mean to say, regardless if the trigger was a minor one. Stressors seem to build on each other leading to greater and greater expressions of anger. This is how your emotional state clouds your thinking, creating roadblocks to resolving conflicts. So, what do you do? Awareness is once again the answer. Once you identify the source of stress that caused you to react as you did, then you can problem-solve.

Fifteen Fundamental Rules of Anger

1. Anger is a Natural Feeling

Anger that is justified and appropriately expressed can be a good thing. I'm not a Bible Scholar, but I recall reading about acts of anger by those who are otherwise pacifists like Moses and Jesus Christ. There are two instances that stand out in my mind. When Moses descended from the mountain after receiving the ten commandments, he discovered the Israelites celebrating and worshipping idols made of gold. He was beside himself. In a fit of rage, he threw down the Commandments, breaking them, in response to his disgust of the people that he was leading to the land of milk and honey. Jesus, on the other hand, went to Jerusalem during Passover. Upon entering the temple, he discovered that it was also a place to sell goods and animals for sacrifice. In anger, Jesus overturned the tables, dumped out the money, and drove out the animals. These examples show that anger is an okay feeling in some circumstances. Whenever a true injustice is committed against us, or something that we believe in and have strong feelings for, or even against someone who is important to us, anger is often the result. It's just natural.

People often associate adjectives like bad, terrible, and evil with anger, and then adopt this belief into their core values. Society discourages showing the feeling of anger, when in actuality, it is normal and there is nothing wrong with this feeling. The problem lies in how it is expressed. Numerous times in the day, the feeling of anger crops up in our minds and bodies. This does not make us bad people, but a part of being human. People often associate anger with the intense feeling of rage, thinking these are one and the same. Nothing could be further from the truth. While rage may be exhibited by most of us at one time or another, there are some people who seem to be more prone to outbursts of rage than others. Dealing with withdrawal from a drug may lower your resistance to stressors and make you more susceptible to rage. Then there are those individuals whose rage can be the result of abuse that occurred during their childhood. Teenagers coming from dysfunctional homes may also exhibit this behavior. Because of unfortunate events, which result in pain and unresolved issues, these individuals have trouble coping with their deep-rooted feelings.

Imagine that you are sitting around your fireplace in your living room, enjoying the warmth of the flames, conversing with good friends, and having a wonderful evening. Your friends leave and you retire for the night, leaving the fire unattended. Suddenly, a small spark escapes the fireplace, starting a small fire. Before long, the fire grows and the whole living room becomes engulfed in flames. Fortunately, you have working smoke alarms and get out of the house safely. By the time the fire truck arrives, your whole house is on fire. This visualization demonstrates how anger can start out as a mild irritation and grow to intense rage which, of course, becomes beyond your control. Destructive forces are then inevitable.

Expression of anger is also developmentally related. For instance, anger is one of the first emotions that newborn babies show at birth. The redness in their face and loud cries quickly bring us to their demands. Babies do not try to conceal their anger when they are going through discomfort because this is a natural response for them and the only way they know how to or can express their pain of hunger, wet diaper, etc. And it is what we expect them to do. For every developmental stage, there is a new set of rules on how to express anger.

Teens have the ability for abstract thinking such as being able to imagine a situation and a response. As they mature, they can identify underlying feelings and apply them in problem-solving. But most importantly teens, like older adults, have the ability to delay recognition of uncomfortable feelings, and then work through it later. The ability to delay is a developmental milestone. This is also when anger can actually be good if handled properly, and we will discuss more about this later.

In actuality, anger can be very useful if it is understood and applied with awareness and insight. Since anger is natural, the important issue is how you react. Be proactive by learning to identify your *anger triggers* and *stressors* so that you are prepared. Certain people, a situation, or something that someone says are possible triggers that may ignite your temper. There are times when this feeling is definitely justified, but it can be managed to reduce in frequency and intensity if you are prepared. Once you are aware of the anger, you can identify the underlying feeling to gain an understanding of the problem, and then do thoughtful reasoning about how to respond.

2. Anger Causes Physical Changes in Your Body

Have you ever been so mad that you could feel your heart pounding in your chest or have a loud ringing in your ears? Have you ever noticed, when you're mad, that you have a tendency to get hot in the face, even perspire, as you get madder and madder? Muscles become tense. Breathing becomes rapid and shallow. It becomes harder to think and form logical thoughts. You might find a sharp rise in your blood pressure. All of these changes occur when you become angry and, the angrier you get, the more these physical changes increase.

The autonomic nervous system is responsible for these changes. This system starts the "fight/flight response" by releasing hormones. The chemicals of epinephrine and norepinephrine are released in your body and this provides the energy that propels you into action. These chemicals give you added strength. The physical changes that occur can actually help you if your anger does not get too intense, but when your anger level gets too high, these changes hurt your ability to think and act.

Physical changes are a signal to alert you that the feeling of anger is on the rise. If you ignore these warning signs, chances are you will let your anger out in a harmful way. These signs include: clinched fists, rapid breathing, gritted teeth, loud voice, butterflies in the stomach, red face, and pounding heart. In this condition, you can do a lot of harm to yourself and others. Don't fall into the trap. What are your warning signs? Can you catch yourself while you are undergoing the early stages? By recognizing these early warning signs, you can save yourself a lot of trouble.

3. Anger Creates Energy in Our Body That Cannot Be Destroyed

Now that you know some of the physical changes that occur inside your body when anger is present, look deeper into your imagination and picture blood being pumped out at a rapid pace to all of your bodily organs, sugar pouring into your system, adrenaline being released throughout your body—all to help prepare you for a response, an action. All of these changes create energy inside your body to help you deal with the anger trigger, what made you angry.

Anger generates energy that cannot be destroyed; it doesn't go away on its own. This energy remains trapped in your body until you find a way to release it. The choice becomes yours: Do you let the energy out by expressing it in some way or do you ignore it, allowing it to be buried deep inside of you?

You could hit someone, break something, or yell. If you do any of these, you will probably be in a lot of trouble. A better choice and more beneficial to you could be physical activities—walk, jog, clean your room, build something. You could also engage in mental activity to counteract your adrenalin rush—puzzles, reading, studying. If you choose to ignore and bury your anger, there are consequences. This energy will weaken the mind and have a negative effect physically. You'll suffer in the long run. This is called repressed anger and can harm almost any part of your body, and influence your feelings and thoughts. This buried anger can be a related factor to headaches, ulcers, rashes, heart problems, cancer, and can leave you vulnerable to colds and other illnesses.

4. Anger Can Be Both Harmful and Helpful

We touched on this earlier, but how can anger possibly be beneficial to you? We all have a pretty good idea of the detrimental effects, especially anger that is not dealt with in an acceptable way. How anger affects the mind, the body, and the spirit, how it harms you, and how it helps is important to know. If you fail to understand how your anger works, and are unsuccessful at expressing it appropriately, you are on track for some hard times. According to the WebMD website, 75-90% of patient visits to the doctor are stress-related ailments or complaints. Anger is certainly a part of this because stress makes us more likely to become angry. As noted earlier with repressed anger, medical issues may occur. High blood pressure, heart disease, muscle tension, headaches, stomach distress, diarrhea, constipation, anorexia nervosa, peptic ulcers, are all physical reactions characteristic of individuals who are anger-prone. Don't hurt yourself with your anger. Be aware that repressed anger is also exhibited by behaviors like hoarding, greed, and being a workaholic. The feeling of anger not only attacks your body but affects the people around you. Making friends and losing friends are both obstacles for angry people who tend to be lonely and isolated. As noted earlier, no one likes to be around them. Most importantly, how we express our anger will determine whether beneficial or harmful consequences will result.

We can try many ways to get control of our lives by reducing our stress and anger. Healthy activities include, but are not limited to: exercise, studying, learning a new skill, participating in a sport, reading, helping others in need, and yes, even cleaning your room. Unhealthy activities include drinking, gossiping, backbiting, wallowing in feeling hopeless, and hurting others. As with repressed anger, chronic anger patterns can lead to serious and severe medical problems and addictions.

Following is a list of some harmful and helpful effects of anger. Please review them and see if you can come up with some ideas of your own to add.

HARMFUL	HELPFUL
Increase in negative physical issues: Headache, ulcers, heart problems, sleep problems, etc.	Acts as a signal that a problem exists

Loss of friends, social problems	Motivates a person to solve problems
Can lead to depression—anger turned inward	Provides energy to help things get done
Can lead to alcohol/drug problems	Delays painful feelings until you are ready to cope with them
Can lead to expulsion from school or incarceration (jail)	Prevents people from taking advantage of you
Can lead to job loss	Provides you with motivation to combat social injustice
Traffic accidents	
Abuse or hurting others	
Depression	

5. Anger Makes Us Aware That a Problem Exists

Our anger has many advantages. One of them is its ability to warn us that there is a problem in our life that needs to be identified and solved. After all, how is it possible to work on a problem if you don't know it exists? Perhaps this is why some people live in denial. They would rather push their problems off to the side than take the emotional energy necessary to face them, so avoidance is their solution. But lying hidden in their subconscious is a sea of unresolved feelings just waiting to escape, to come back with a vengeance. When problems are covered up and ignored, denial is the defense mechanism used to protect their self-esteem. People who use denial often develop a faulty pattern of dealing with their feelings, leading to various physical and social problems as mentioned earlier. Problems stack up, making it overwhelming just to make simple decisions. Remember, the problem is about you, not something outside of yourself. When you feel angry, there is something that is causing the pain. It is affecting your very soul. Whatever you do, action needs to be taken—one that is good for you and other people.

But how do you handle your anger without creating resistance and resentment? If you attempt to bully or scare people, you may get them to cooperate with you for the moment. However, in the long run, they will ignore and avoid you. An alternative solution is to develop good communication and problem-solving skills. When you clearly see what the real problem is, you can move past your anger and on to rational decision-making by reviewing your options to find a satisfactory solution. Simply be aware of the warning signs, evaluate the situation, and move quickly to problem-solving.

6. You Have a Choice about How to Handle Anger

Anger and aggression are two words that are sometimes used interchangeably. This is definitely not correct and nothing can be further from the truth. Anger can be described as a complex emotion. Even for the calmest of individuals, anger pops up in their life frequently. Aggression, on the other hand, is different. It is an act that we choose, that is intentional. While anger is more difficult to prevent since it is natural and part of our emotional make-up, aggression is a form of revenge—a behavioral reaction, an intention to hurt or do harm to another, and *it* is definitely controllable. Aggressive people make up excuses for their actions. They might be pushy, insulting, raise their voice, yell at others, destroy property, and in extreme cases, physically harm someone. Oh yes! Let's not forget about threats, especially threats to harm others that are meant to cause fear. As an educator, I found these occurrences prevalent in both middle and high schools. These aggressors could definitely turn a good day into a bad one. Some students used intimidation to meet some inadequacy of their own. Perhaps it was a character flaw or a gap in their moral development. Whatever the reason, these students made life in a school environment miserable for those around them. Obviously, something was wrong that made them behave this way, and they too needed an intervention.

Fortunately, instead of aggression, most students chose to channel their anger into more productive pursuits. Sports was one of these channels. Football, basketball, and wrestling provided the release of energy and unblocked any stored-up anger and frustration. Academic pursuits such as projects, research, and debate also provided an outlet for emotions, including anger. Opportunities or successful pursuits are especially plentiful for students.

As people grow older, they develop a more sophisticated view of how they perceive the world, which sadly can include distortions and misconceptions. Denial can be one of these misconceptions. They justify their aggression by claiming they had no choice in the matter; that it is not their fault. They continue to blame others as a way to live their lives. In reality, they are failing to accept responsibility for their own feelings and actions, excusing themselves to the detriment of others. While people have a right to make a choice about how to express themselves, they do not have the right to inflict unjustified hurt. There is some question as to which is more harmful: demeaning words or physical acts. In some instances, words are more painful, especially if they are in the form of gossiping, backbiting, name-calling, or belittling. Words said in anger can have lasting effects, even over many years. You might never even forget the hurtful things that were said. Remember this fact: When you lose control of your anger, but you speak anyway, others as well as you may pay the price.

To ensure you make the best choice of how to respond to anger when it occurs, you will need a plan in advance that you can follow, listing various situations that could result in making you angry. This action prepares you for handling future encounters appropriately. Remember: *The key to learning anger-coping strategies is to get your needs met without hurting other people.* If you feel you want to harm or hurt another person or living thing, your anger is escaping beyond the boundary of acceptability. It is a signal that you need to slow down and take an inner-look at yourself. It is a warning that you need to solve a problem. Ask yourself weekly: What am I doing with my anger? How am I responding to it? Is it good for me? Is it fair to others?

When people have gone through traumatic circumstances earlier in their lives, the anger that originates from these occurrences needs a different method of anger management. As mentioned earlier, these types of occurrences include, but are not limited to abandonment, physical abuse, and emotional abuse. Seeking professional help is the best way to deal with chronic anger if it becomes out of control, but first, try to work on the underlying problems when you feel the surge of anger coming into your thoughts.

As noted, when we encounter the stressors of life, we have a choice on how we will respond. That response will be influenced by our thoughts and words, and those thoughts and words will affect what we believe. What we believe has a way of becoming reality. Be careful. Think before you act, then react.

7. People Don't Make You Mad— You Choose to Get Mad

"David makes me so angry. I just can't stand that guy! Who does he think he is anyway? He is always acting so smug and sarcastic." "Why does Sally always have to put me in a bad mood?" "It's Connie's fault that we are having a bad time. She always has to have everything her way. She is so annoying to be around." "All that Mike does is gripe and complain. He makes me so mad!" "Larry is such a tightwad. When it comes to contributing to dinner, he never has money for the meal. He also had to borrow money to get into the theatre. He is such a freeloader. I get so mad when he pulls the 'poor boy' act." Do any of these comments sound like something you might say or think? Do you blame others for your anger and upset feelings? Is it their fault? Why do we blame others? By believing that someone else is responsible for your anger and hurt, you play the part of a victim. People play the victim role because they do not have to accept responsibility for how they express their anger. For victims, it is easier to avoid their own pain and pass it along to another person, usually through complaints, gossiping, or backbiting. Just remember that anger comes from *your* thoughts. Take responsibility and make sure you are aware of them because they will determine your actions.

When growing up, I remember getting upset with several of the boys in my class—Steve, Michael, Ed, and Bill. They were so good at sports and I was just the opposite. In football, I always had to be the rusher and never got the chance to catch the ball or be the quarterback. In baseball, my duty always became right field. That, of course, is where they usually put the worst player on the team. My batting was even worse. Either the ball or the bat did not seem big enough. Striking out was what I did best. Imagine how humiliating all of this was for me, and maybe you can even identify. Whenever there were two outs and I came up to the plate, everyone got their gloves and prepared to take the field, even before I completed my batting appearance. I blamed my classmates for my anger and humiliation. My only salvation in grade school came from using my legs. Luckily, I was the fastest runner in our school. Now, that was one sport where I was the first person to be picked, as we would always have two teams racing against each other. But being the best at racing just wasn't good enough for me. I was uncoordinated, which didn't go along with athletics. I felt inferior, like I was the victim. All of my perceived power was given to the other boys in my class. If only I knew then what I know now.

The more I blamed others for my inadequacies, the more I felt drained and trapped in my misery. In place of blaming my anger on the other kids and internalizing it in self-punishing feelings toward myself, I needed to give myself a dose of personal growth. I needed an adult or a peer to help me improve my skills. Looking outside of myself at the other boys only made me miserable and not able to face the problem. It was *their* fault for my anger, and my unhappiness. The lesson I later learned in life (too bad I didn't learn it earlier when I was younger) was that we are responsible for our own thoughts, our feelings, our actions. We then have a choice of whether they work for or against us. What was the message before? *I am responsible for my own anger. No one makes me mad; I choose to get mad.*

This is also so important to remember: Do not expect other people to make changes in their lives to accommodate what you want! That is not a realistic expectation. No one is responsible for making another person happy. There is a general rule in all interpersonal encounters: There will be times when each of you go away from a situation without feeling satisfied. Sometimes people's needs clash. Just because you want to feel good and avoid pain doesn't mean that other people do not have the same desire to feel good and avoid discomfort. You are responsible for your thoughts, your feelings, and your actions just as others are for theirs. Don't be a victim. Don't stagnate, refusing to take responsibility for how you choose to feel.

8. Anger Tends to Create More Anger

Professionals in the field of mental health used to believe that allowing a person to physically express or vent their anger would rid them of destructive force. They encouraged clients to express their anger, let out their rage, and free themselves of their pain. Hitting a pillow, punching a bag, and kicking were common practices. This might work for people who have been severely abused in the past, but for the most part, this method of thinking is no longer believed to be true because the person is still practicing aggression. Now it is widely believed that if you let your anger out on another person without exercising any self-control, you will become more, not less, angry and then that person will become upset with you. It then forms a cycle. You instigate the aggression to make the other person feel pain, to suffer. Then that person retaliates to cause you pain, to make you suffer, perhaps even more. It would be wiser not to say anything or do anything until you regain self-control. If you try to get back at someone for what they said or did, anger increases for both of you. Think about what your actions are like when you let out your angry feelings on others. If you hit them, they will probably hit you back. When you yell at them, cuss, or call them names, they will probably yell back, cuss and call you names in return. When you blame them, they will get defensive and communication stops. Even the people who might be intimidated by you and won't fight back will find other ways to get even in the future.

When you yell, hit, or blame others, you are being aggressive. This is not a good way to handle your anger or other uncomfortable feelings. Aggressive people are described as a bully, manipulative, pushy, and demanding. If you do aggressive things, you are trying to make other people feel they are bad or wrong for not giving you what you need. By being aggressive, you are trying to choose for them what to feel without taking their needs into consideration.

There is a difference between being angry and being an angry person. One is a temporary feeling and the other becomes a characteristic. For example, on the highway you might find the angry and aggressive person always honks his horn at other people, yelling and cursing at them. I can't say that I haven't occasionally engaged in some yelling myself when a sudden and brief negative situation occurs, but the anger is gone when the encounter is finished. On the other hand, an angry person yells, curses and honks routinely. The angry person always has to be right, or at least most of the time, and there is no way you can win an argument with him. People try to avoid angry and aggressive individuals when they can because their anger can be contagious, and it is just unpleasant to be around them. The other extreme of being aggressive is to be passive. If you are passive, you will not say anything to offend anyone. On the outside, you appear agreeable to what other people want you to do. They might refer to you as a nice or good person, and describe you as shy and somewhat quiet. On the inside, you might feel helpless, with none of your needs being met. By being passive, you allow others to choose for you. You lose focus of your identity. You internalize your anger or, in other words, become angry at yourself for letting it happen. If you choose to yell, call people names, hit someone, or become passive, you will get angrier and have less self-control for the moment and over time. As said before, if you show your anger, the other person often gets angry too and problems arise, stopping communication. When that happens, your opportunity to problem-solve is greatly reduced. If you let other people take advantage of you by being passive, your own self-esteem will be eroded and you will become repressed and suffer its effects, also noted earlier. Both aggression and passiveness build up to an angry disposition within you. Anger can take up a lot of your time and use up a lot of your positive energy if you let it. Look out for yourself and the other person. Don't give in to the destructive forces of anger. Reduce the anger, don't increase it. Let it go! Let it flow!

9. Anger Can Protect Us Against Painful Feelings

Anger is very much a "gateway" feeling. Once you get past it, you enter a world of uncomfortable and painful feelings. A choice is then bestowed upon us, one that we must accept. We can choose to deal with the underlying feeling (why we became angry) immediately, we can wait to deal with it at a later date, or we can ignore it entirely. However, before we can choose any of our options, we need to be aware of and identify the underlying feeling, and this might be difficult. The more intense our feeling is, the more time it takes to identify, reflect and problem-solve. Anger allows you to do just that when it blocks the painful feeling and increases the time necessary to cope with it. This makes anger quite useful and keeps you from making decisions that will hurt you and others, but it is vital to express it without too much time passing.

Take this scenario for example: You found out that one of your friends was having a get-together and you were not invited. Everyone else will probably be there. Why were you excluded? You are angry! Why? Perhaps you feel rejected. A lot of your other friends were included, but not you. Maybe you feel betrayed because you thought you had a closer relationship with the person hosting the event. How about dejected? You really do want to go. You do your analysis of the situation, and then the moment arises of how and when you express your anger. Before you react, make sure you are in control and then take

appropriate action. Express your anger, but be sure to direct it toward your friend who neglected to invite you. Do not make the mistake of blaming or taking it out on others. Remember, anger is acting as a shield for your protection. When comfortable, stand up for yourself. Do not let your friend mistreat you unjustly, or purposely harm you. Come away with some sort of satisfaction. In this situation, you decide to use assertiveness. Even though you are nervous and have butterflies in your stomach, you go over to your friend's house, ask them why you were not invited and tell them how it makes you feel. Be ready to accept their explanation. Hopefully, you will gain insight from the incident, allowing you to improve your reaction quicker and more efficiently if this type of issue happens again.

The emotion of anger is *always* subject to an uncomfortable or painful feeling. Anger, therefore, acts as your protector, as strange as that sounds. The bottom line is that your anger plays an instrumental role when it comes to recognizing hidden, subconscious feelings. By having the choice to express or delay them, more control is given which keeps you from being overwhelmed. If used correctly, anger definitely has its advantages.

To explain how this works, first a signal goes off inside your mind and body. You become irritable and angry, and you don't exactly know why. But what you do know, consciously or unconsciously, is that anger is acting as a warning, indicating a problem. It's a question of: What are you feeling and why? You realize something is going on because feelings such as disappointment, guilt, jealousy, rejection, and embarrassment precede anger.

The process of learning to identify and then express uncomfortable feelings in a healthy manner is difficult if not practiced regularly. Instead, to avoid future problems, work through these feelings and don't ignore them. This allows you to problem-solve and find the best solution. If you face hurt because you have been criticized or rejected, then you must own the feeling and find a way to deal with it. This might mean telling the other person what it was that hurt you as in the scenario of your friend not inviting you to a get-together. Maybe you'll need to take a time-out and get your thoughts and feelings under control before you talk with the person about the problem. Whatever you do, don't REPRESS or ignore your feelings. Deal with it in your conscious mind. Don't let time go by and allow it to hide in your subconscious or unconscious mind. That leads to further trouble.

10. Anger is a Reaction to Hurt, Loss, or Fear

If you take a moment to reflect, you will realize that *all* anger is a result of hurt, loss or fear. When you get your feelings hurt because someone belittles you or puts you down, do you get angry? It is hard for people to accept criticism and negativity from others. When a good friend moves away or you get kicked off the track team, or fired from your job, anger tends to creep into your mind and body. Even when someone close to you dies, it is natural to feel anger. Why? It is difficult for people to cope with losses in their lives. In short, it is hard to feel "hurt."

Grief, which is a cycle, is common to all of us, and consists of a variety of emotions, including anger. In grief, it is no surprise that the greater the love for the person, the greater the effect of the loss. But it is the role of grief to help us heal and grow as human beings when we do experience a loss, as long as we flow through the process and do not get stuck in it. There is danger if you can't work through it so let it flow through your being the way it is supposed to do. If you block or ignore it, grief sets you up for some complicated problems. Do note, however, *you never get over the pain when a loved one passes on to the next world. The pain only lessens with time.* We will discuss grief again later in this chapter.

The grieving process does not need to be confined to the death of loved ones. Anytime a significant loss occurs in our lives, the grieving process must begin with recognition and end with acknowledgment of the loss. How long does this last? This depends on the value of what you lost. At first, you might be in shock; you can't believe that it really happened. It is difficult to come to grips with the loss. Then anger sets in with questions like, "Why did it have to happen?" Action can only be taken once you come to terms with what has happened and that it is reality, but be aware that waves of grief can affect you for an undetermined amount of time during the process. Your feelings may sometimes overtake you, and this is only natural, but it is important to face them and not avoid them when you are ready. Let yourself heal over time and understand you are not always going to feel this way. Grief is a common occurrence in life and the grieving process is part of the human condition.

If people don't understand someone or something, they often feel threatened and afraid. Then they become angry. Fear of failure in school can result in anger and acting-out behavior, just as it did with many of the special education students with whom I worked in public schools. I can only imagine the fear and pain these students must have gone through, knowing they couldn't learn as easily as their peers. They had to struggle each day in an environment that did not enhance their talents. I'm sure they used their anger and defense mechanisms to help cope with their fears of possible failure.

Imagine, too, the effects of significant social trauma for the young children who survive mass shootings in schools. Each time they hear a gunshot or a loud noise, they may cower in fear. What about the citizens in war-ravaged countries? Each day, they come out of their homes, knowing of the possibility that danger is present and the loss of a family member is always a possibility. The same kind of fear might be felt in inner-city slums where the violence of gang activity is a constant threat. Fear is another strong emotion that is part of us and can lead to anger problems. As with other fears, don't avoid it...just feel it...work through it.

11. The Greater the Disappointment, the Greater the Anger

You finally got a date with one of the popular cheerleaders, the one whose attention you have been trying to get for the past month. This is going to be one fine evening—dinner, then a movie. The day comes. Your spirits are sky-high and then she calls and breaks the date. She gives you a flimsy excuse. You're not quite sure if she is telling the truth. Talk about being deflated!

The setting is a youth detention center. What a terrible place to be, confined with little freedom. Five months have passed and your parole release time is rapidly approaching. One week before you are to be released, a counselor and administrator want to meet with you. What's up? This can't be good. They inform you they believe you are still having difficulty following the expected behavior and your time in the facility has been extended. You are devastated and practically in a fit of rage.

This fundamental rule is obvious to us all: When people look forward to anticipated events or rewards and they aren't fulfilled, the result is often frustration and disappointment. On the outside, you might get angry. Inside, you get that sick feeling in your stomach. Anger covers up the real feelings. When people promise you something or tell you what they are going to do for you, it is natural to be filled with hope and anticipation. When it doesn't happen, your hope comes crashing down and disappointment takes over. The same is true when we are expecting a reward or something that we earned. Your attitudes, beliefs, and expectations are all contributors to making you angry when things are thwarted.

Everyone learns a set of rules about how people should and should not act. What rules do you value that everyone should live by? Do you believe that the world should be fair to you? Do you expect other people to give you what you want? Try not to set yourself up for disappointments, and keep your expectations realistic for yourself and for others.

12. Compassion and Forgiveness Reduce Anger

Compassion and forgiveness for others requires you to take a moment, step back, and try to put yourself in the other person's shoes. These are two virtues that help define us on a higher level as human beings, and they are mutually beneficial to both parties.

Compassion is a virtue that, when used, can reduce anger and leave a sense of calm.

Realizing that the angry individual is suffering from some form of pain, the use of empathy and understanding can diffuse the situation. Of course, this intervention requires a strong dose of self-esteem within yourself, protecting you from the bitterness and temporary hateful attitude of the angry person. What is not practiced at this time is problem-solving and analysis. Instead, caring and concern for the misfortune of others is the goal. Active listening is a useful skill in showing compassion. This involves the reflection of the thoughts and feelings of the angry individual by providing feedback, demonstrating that you are listening to help them handle their emotions. Speaking less and not judging are critical. Give them a chance to talk out their feelings, concerns, and problems with the ultimate goal to support them in some manner, no matter how bad things are. Sincerity must be the primary driving force and the basis of your intentions because, without it, your actions will have little effect or may backfire and make the situation worse.

Forgiveness isn't easy and takes more effort than compassion, but *forgiveness is not to be confused with forgetting.* "Why should I forgive them? They should apologize to me! After all, I'm the person who got hurt and am upset. In fact, I think they should be punished for hurting me!" Does that sound like a common reaction? Forgiveness is a difficult practice to learn. This is especially true when you have been betrayed by someone close to you. Forgiveness is a choice that, if you choose it, can restore inner peace, and help you heal so that you can move on. That is important because energy is consumed the longer you take to forgive, or if you decide forgiveness is not the course of action. Remember, a grudge can lead to damaging and long-term effects because negative emotions are stored up without a release, causing possible problems with personal relationships or physical ailments in the body. Without forgiveness, both parties tend to suffer over time. For each situation, you must decide if you are going to forgive, hold on to a grudge, or be somewhere between. But as noted earlier, when you forgive others, you don't let them off the hook for what they did; they are still responsible for their actions. In the future, just watch the forgiven person carefully so you won't be hurt a second time. Regard them with caution, but attempt to free yourself of grudges, hatred, and self-pity.

Self-forgiveness may be a more important skill than learning how to forgive others. When you say or do things you regret, you may be holding onto feelings that are still bothering you. Who hasn't committed an act they wished they could change? None of us are perfect. Shame and guilt are often the result when you refuse to forgive yourself—two feelings that are buried in your soul, leading to more negative emotions in the future. Coming to terms with these feelings is important for your emotional well-being. Otherwise, damage can erode your self-esteem and allow you to sink deeper into despair. Self-forgiveness is a step in the right direction to help you begin to make peace within yourself. The enemies, shame and guilt, are attacked by your conscious mind when you can acknowledge them through training to replace negative thoughts with positive thoughts. When you begin to feel better about yourself, people are attracted to you, making it possible for you to tap into your virtues to help others.

13. Feelings Are Temporary

You are driving along and someone cuts you off and honks his horn. Anger sets in because you feel that you are being treated unjustly. Retaliation comes to mind. You might use profanity, honk your horn repeatedly, or follow his car very closely to make him feel uncomfortable. A few miles down the road, you forget the other guy and continue on with your day, feeling good, thinking about other things.

Painful feelings, along with the pleasurable ones, are normally both temporary. That is the way our Creator made us. No one wants to be in pain. Feelings, however, change throughout the day—alternating, giving us a chance to grow, to rest. So give it time and tell yourself, "Whatever this current feeling is, it will pass. The other person does not have to change for me to feel good." Resume your day with a positive attitude feeling good about yourself, walking with confidence, smiling, greeting others, and you are on your way.

As discussed previously, feelings originate from our thoughts. How many times have we misinterpreted an event or the intentions of another? We might even hold on to this interpretation for years, when it isn't even true. Therefore, if we are able to change the way we think, we can alleviate some problems that are a result. Being able to change our thoughts is a skill that doesn't come easily. Sometimes, it seems that thoughts occur automatically and you just can't turn them off. If we can't change, or have difficulty changing our thoughts, we can still achieve some satisfaction knowing that they will go away or lessen in time depending on their severity. Don't be held captive by your feelings. Find a way to ensure they remain temporary, even if it requires the help of a professional.

14. Repressed Feelings Come Back to Haunt Us

A widely held view is that depression is nothing more than anger turned inward. If this is true, why not find ways to release your anger and get it out of your system? This, however, may be too simplistic of an explanation because of other factors that are involved. Whatever the case, no one wants to experience undesirable feelings, especially depression, yet, everyone has them. Problems multiply when you decide to dismiss or repress them. Long-term repressed feelings can cause serious harm. What do we mean by repressed feelings? The word repressed means that you bury them, fail to own up, to become blind to them. In the short term, a conscious delay (suppression) could be beneficial. Anger can protect us from painful feelings as discussed earlier. In the long term, negative feelings that you do not allow to come to your conscious mind, ones that you refuse to confront, poison your sense of being. To be afraid of painful feelings and pretend that they don't exist results in a whole range of problems awaiting you down the road.

Negative emotions are the stressors in life. Talk to someone and share your pain with a person who is mature, compassionate, and kind. Negative emotions apply pressure on us and it is so easy to want to ignore them, brush them off to the side, or put them on the fringes of our memory. Storing them in the recesses of the subconscious and unconscious mind, though, does have destructive and damaging consequences. Deep-rooted, long-term repressed feelings often require professional help later in life to handle the distortions. However, the main dilemma with repressed feelings is that they lead to denial, which blocks insight.

15. Virtues and Spirituality Define Who We Are

Spiraling through the universe, with our bodies bound to earth, our souls are in preparation for the journey of eternity. Even if you don't believe in having a soul, there is a spiritual aspect to humans. The law of thermodynamics states that energy cannot be created or destroyed. Humans are energy and energy never dies. It only transforms. I believe it is our nature to yearn for spiritual intervention. Our goal is to discover our own individual paths, to find that glimpse, that connection, that lifeline.

Giving service to others leads us closer to our destiny—one of peace and contentment. Unity, justice, truthfulness, faith, and love are virtues that prepare us for the transformation that will evolve when our spirit separates from the body. Entering the sea of lights, the realities of the next world will become evident. The question becomes: What can we do to make our present existence a better one and prepare ourselves for what follows? We have been blessed with wonderful minds and powerful souls, and a vast range of feelings that make up our emotional selves. We use these in our interpersonal relationships with others. When you put the mind, the feelings, the virtues, and the soul together, you have a wonderful and powerful human being. The virtues are all inter-connected, and together they define us as a person. If everyone in the world would work to improve on the characteristic attributes of these virtues, the world would definitely be more united and take a step forward in creating a spiritual, ever-advancing civilization.

Ways You Express Your Anger: Self-Evaluation

This is an exercise to discover how you express your painful and uncomfortable feelings. To what degree do you express them in "helpful ways" and "not helpful ways?" Begin this exercise by looking over the useful ways to show anger and then rate each of the 10 as follows:

1 = seldom

2 = once a week

3 = several times a week

4 = daily

When you are finished with the helpful ways, begin working on the not helpful ways, using the same rating scale.

HELPFUL EXPRESSIONS OF ANGER

_____ 1) Take a time-out

This activity allows people to get control of their feelings so they can act in a fair and just manner towards themselves and others. The time-out could include taking a short walk, reading a book, listening to music.

_____ 2) Exercise/do physical activities

These activities can range from doing aerobics...to riding a bike...to gardening...to walking the dog...to playing sports, etc.

_____ 3) Talk to a friend

Having a good friend or friends to talk to is one of the many blessings in life. A good friend is there to listen, to be empathetic, to be non-judgmental.

_____ 4) Study/learn something new

When people read, study or learn something new, they are channeling their feelings in a helpful way.

_____ 5) Be assertive

Individuals own their feelings and opinions by making "I" statements like, "I am troubled because..." State your opinion in a calm manner.

_____ 6) Use artistic expressions

Poetry, creative writing, drawing, ceramics, singing, and playing a musical instrument are creative examples of activities that help people express their feelings.

_____ 7) Help someone in need

Taking care of people when they are sick, giving them rides to the store, giving to charities, being kind to others, listening to them when they need to talk are examples of helping others

_____ 8) See the other person's point of view

Everyone interprets an event differently. Put yourself in the other person's shoes and try to view the situation from their eyes

_____ 9) Change your expectations

When you expect something to happen and it doesn't, you become unhappy and disappointed. Be flexible, find an alternative.

_____ 10) Work to make change

When something happens that is not fair or is unjust, advocate for change. Mobilize a petition drive or protest, for example.

Harmful Ways to Express Anger

1) Belittling

　　_____ Call people names

　　_____ Yell at other people

　　_____ Use profanity

　　_____ Make rude and sarcastic comments

　　_____ Use racial or cultural slurs

　　_____ _____

2) Arguments

　　_____ With significant other

　　_____ With adults

　　_____ With parents

　　_____ With brothers/sisters

　　_____ With children

　　_____ With strangers

　　_____ _____

3) Threats

_____ To friends

_____ To adults

_____ To parents

_____ To brother/sisters

_____ To children

____ _____

4) Passive/aggressive behavior

_____ Pout

_____ Tattle (tell on others)

_____ Gossip (talk behind a person's back)

_____ Be late for appointments

_____ Forget to do chores/duties

____ _____

5) Physical harm to self

_____ Hit walls/windows/objects

_____ Try to hurt myself

_____ Attempt suicide

____ _____

6) Physical harm to others

　　_____ Hit/kick/push

　　_____ Pull hair

　　_____ Bite

　　_____ Scream

　　_____ Cause a disruption or make a scene

_____   _____

7) Physical misuse of things/animals

　　_____ Break things

　　_____ Throw things

　　_____ Slam doors

　　_____ Be cruel to animals

_____   _____

8) Avoidance

　　_____ Stay away, avoid the person

　　_____ Passive/shy

　　_____ Lie

　　_____ Consume alcohol/take drugs

　　_____ Procrastinate

9) Projection

_____ Blame others for your anger ("You make me mad.")

_____ Feel others should be punished for making you mad

10) Displacement

_____ I'm mad at my boss so I take it out on my family or others

_____ I'm mad at my parents so I take it out on my teacher

_____ _____

Evaluate Yourself

Now that you have rated yourself on this exercise, tally your responses and determine your patterns. Do you channel your feelings into ways that will help you? Or do you channel your feelings into ways that harm you or lead to further problems? Next, give it to a friend or adult and ask them to rate how they think you express yourself. Once you have determined the patterns of your anger, decide which harmful patterns are you willing to work on. Which helpful patterns are you willing to practice? Set a goal or two for yourself and work towards accomplishing them.

Ways to Control Your Anger

1. Breathe Deeply

This strategy is natural, almost automatic, and very simplistic. We learn early in life that taking a deep breath or breathing deeply is a very quick way to help us begin to handle stress. You can see people using this technique regularly. In the morning when the alarm goes off, you may take a deep breath. You may not want to get out of bed, so taking some more deep breaths is a natural reaction. Basketball players, when the pressure is on them while standing at the free throw line, often bounce the ball, take a few deep breaths for concentration, and hopefully shoot the ball through the net. Children, while roughhousing in the living room accidentally break their mom's good lamp, might take some deep breaths as they get up the courage to own up to this unfortunate event. In high school, when a guy has a date with a girl for the first time and wants to make a good impression, he will likely take several deep breaths to alleviate some of his anxiety before knocking on her door.

Whenever stress becomes intense, focused breathing helps to relieve some of the tension. This technique, when performed properly, requires one to breathe in through the nose and out through the mouth. As you breathe out, pair it with a word in your mind to maintain control like "relax, stay calm," or "chill." Come up with your own word or words. You might think as you breathe in, I am letting the fresh air enter my body. As you breathe out, you might think, I am releasing the tension that has built up. The one I have been using lately when I inhale is let success and positive energy fill my mind and body. Then, let the failure and negative energy be exhaled. Be creative. Use the word or phrase that works best for you. Try closing your eyes, take several deep breaths to free your mind, and focus on the positive.

The only problem with this technique is just remembering to use it. Do you wear a necklace? This may act as a good reminder to take a deep breath. Each time you feel it, touch it or look at it in a mirror, go ahead and take a deep breath. Get into the habit of using this technique daily. You might also focus on your ring. When you become conscious of it, take a deep breath. Make it a part of your day. Taking a deep breath is both easy and effective. If you know only one anger control technique, make it this one. Mastery is quick and universal, but remember, most people perform this technique without any practice or awareness. Using deep breathing throughout the day becomes a form of mild meditation to help cope with pressure, especially in stressful situations. Make it a habit so that you will know to use it when you need it.

2. Count Backward

Another simple technique you can use to keep your cool when you get angry is counting backward. The power of this strategy lies in the distraction it brings to your thought patterns. When you concentrate on counting backward, it becomes difficult to think about what is making you angry. Put another way, it buys you time to get yourself under control and to respond in a productive, non-impulsive way. To perform this technique, you simply begin to count silently and turn away from the source of the anger. If you look at the person you are angry with, you will probably remain angry or get angrier.

Using the alphabet can also work. Visualizing someone you love or a favorite place is another example. The value of this strategy is that it diverts your attention from the source of your anger, giving you time to regain your composure. This technique, like deep breathing, is easy to implement. Again, you just need to remember to use it, especially in situations where you have pre-planned to use it. A time not to use it is when you are confronted by an authority figure. This action could be interpreted as a sign of disrespect and can have disastrous results. Performing this technique in front of a law enforcement officer, a judge, your boss, a teacher, or your parent would not be a good idea. This would definitely create more anger and more likely increase disciplinary procedures. Not your best option.

3. Think Ahead

Looking into the future, at the consequences of your behavioral actions, is the essence of this technique. The easiest way to understand this concept is to think, *if I do this now, then this is what will happen to me later.* In other words, if you say and do something now that is questionable and not in good taste, then it will have not-so-good consequences in the near future, perhaps the same day if you get caught. An example of a high school student attempting to implement this technique might look something like this: *If I hit him now, then it will feel so good and he deserves it. He might hit back, but I don't care. The consequences of my action might end in my being suspended from school and a harsh reprimand, followed by discipline from my parents like being grounded. They would be furious. Is it worth it?* Thinking ahead requires reasoning and problem-solving. It keeps you from acting impulsively and engaging in activities that could do you harm.

4. Talk to an Adult

An anger management technique that can be useful and is just common sense is to talk to an adult. If you are in middle school or high school, talking to mature, wiser adults can be helpful in sorting out your feelings and providing insight into your anger and the daily problems you encounter. An adult has more experiences to draw from, and can help you be less reactive and more reflective. Realizing that mature, older adults can relate to your feelings and thoughts may provide you with comfort to discuss your situation. Many schools have counselors, social workers and resource personnel who can do just that. But, it is paramount that you have a trusting and respectful relationship with an adult in advance or this strategy may not be as successful as other interventions or techniques. Even adults have other trusted adults they go to when they are dealing with the stresses of what life throws at them. The goal of talking to others is to understand and control your feelings.

5. Talk to a Friend

Talking to our friends is very similar to talking with an adult, but maybe without the same frame of reference and life experiences. The main difference is the trust and loyalty you and your friend have for each other, but at a different level. Most people have a small circle of friends they can reach out to, knowing they will keep their private conversations confidential. Friends are usually easier to talk with, which makes it possible to share your innermost concerns. With a true friend, you can tell them anything, anytime. This makes friendship a valuable asset when you become upset.

Talking to someone that you care for and trust, someone around your own age who is going through similar developmental issues, and who supports you and is always there, makes life easier. Friendship is a powerful anger controller in having a person to talk to who will allow you to let out your pain and your discomfort in a safe and nurturing environment. Having at least one person who listens and understands you is one of the blessings in life. More than one is a bounty.

6. Write a Letter

Your thoughts, written down on a piece of paper, can clarify your anger and other feelings. This might lead to insight, directing you to the source of your problem. This strategy is simply referred to as "write a letter." Don't correct for punctuation, spelling, or grammar. Just express your raw feelings in words. Writing a letter provides an outlet to release your pent-up feelings and make you aware of what they are. After the letter is written, tear it up to avoid further trouble. If another person obtains the letter, it could be used against you. If the person you are angry with sees it, your problem will escalate, compound the issue, and make the matter worse.

There is another alternative to writing a negative letter. This one can be positive in nature.

Shower the object of your anger with praise, as long as you

are being sincere. Mention their strengths and positive qualities. Show appreciation for their friendship. Write down anything that will build up their confidence and reduce problems down the road. Definitely, deliver this one when you are both calm and receptive, either by hand, mail, or whatever seems appropriate. Writing a positive letter, even if it isn't shared, widens your perspective and helps you realize that not everything is negative in your relationship.

If you use writing a letter as a method of anger management, just remember to destroy it if it is negative. There is no reason to hurt another person or make the situation worse.

7. Do Positive Self-Talk

Do you talk to yourself? Talking to yourself is okay and may be good. More importantly, it is what you tell yourself that is critical to your well-being. As a child, my mother would sit for hours painting every day while just talking to herself. This seemed to help with her creative process in designing beautiful paintings on plates and on canvas. Then, too, my Aunt Madeline, whose sport was fishing, would sit on the bank talking to the fish and telling them to get on her line. What can I say? She always came home with a lot of fish and I didn't. Maybe there was a lesson for me to learn—talk to myself and be more positive.

There is documentation that talking to yourself might be high on the list of techniques to assist you in controlling your anger, thoughts, and feelings. Words have an impact on your mind and spirit, whether you speak them silently to yourself or out loud. We know words have a definite effect on our thoughts and our thoughts have a definite effect on our feelings, thus having a definite effect on our actions and influence on the people around us. But, most importantly, spoken or silent words can either limit you or help you to achieve your dreams. When you invest in yourself and put your faith in what you think, feel and say, they become your reality. Make your positive words count.

It has long been known that people live up to or down to what is expected of them. If a person is repeatedly told that he is stupid and dumb, he will eventually act out and play the part of being stupid and dumb. This is the same concept as continually believing you are going to have a bad day, then chances are you will. Dr. David Stoop, a noted California psychologist who wrote *You Are What You Think* explains: "The power released by our Self-Talk is incredible. Not only do our thoughts and words create emotions, but they also have the power to make us well or sick, and to determine our future."

Words spoken by other people also have a definite effect, for benefit or detriment. I have heard people compliment and say good things about me. Their words are full of love. The opposite is also true as people gossip, use racial slurs, downgrade other people's beliefs and religions, and say hateful things when talking about politics. They create a destructive influence on your mind and body, creating toxins the longer you are exposed to them. These negative words darken your spirit, sour your optimism, and deplete your energy. It is important to stop them. Two courses of action are possible. Be assertive and tell the person that his language is making you uncomfortable, or give a choice for the person to please refrain or leave. Let positive words rule your life and avoid the negatives.

Look back in history when Dr. Martin Luther King, Jr., in 1963 on the steps of the Lincoln Memorial, gave a speech during a march on Washington, D.C. that would change a nation. His speech was filled with words that contained frustration and pain, but also faith, ***and*** hope.

> *"So even though we face the difficulties of today and tomorrow, I still have a dream. It is a dream deeply rooted in the American dream. I have a dream that one day this nation will rise up and live out the true meaning of its creed...that all men are created equal. ...I have a dream that one day even the state of Mississippi, a state sweltering with the heat of oppression, will be transformed into an oasis of freedom and justice. I have a dream that my four little children will one day be judged not by the color of*

their skin but by the content of their character. ... And if America is to be a great nation, this must become true. And so let freedom ring..."

Dr. King believed that the future would bring justice and equality to people of all races and religions. We still strive to make that a reality someday.

The words you think and speak, and *how* you think and speak them, have an influence on your everyday life. Be positive and utilize your many gifts and talents. Channel your energy wisely. It takes the same amount of energy whether you think in a positive manner or a negative one. Purge your mind of the negative and replace it with thoughts of optimism. What you think is what you do.   In baseball great Derek Jeter's book, **The Life You Imagine,** he shared a Nike commercial that he remembered about Michael Jordan, a well-known ex-basketball star. He believes that it illustrates how people should make the most of their lives by being positive. The commercial begins with Michael Jordan getting out of his car. He begins to walk toward the locker room and his mind is already engaging in self-talk. "I've missed more than 9,000 shots in my career. I've lost almost 300 games. Twenty-six times, I've been trusted to take the game-winning shot. And missed. I've failed over and over and over again in my life. And that is why I succeed." Note that he takes the negative voice and turns it into something positive. Failure is part of the success formula so you can't be afraid of it. Inevitably, you are going to make mistakes and experience setbacks.

Strengthen your self-talk through awareness and focus. Write down one or two positive affirmations. Practice saying it or them verbally or silently every day for one minute. Get it into your subconscious mind. You can also practice positive self-talk by writing it or visualizing it. Make a poster of the affirmation and put it on the wall. Look at it every day. See it. Believe it. Take action toward it. Tell yourself: "This is the start of a new day. I'm shaking off doubt and negativity. I will be happy and enthusiastic.

Always remember your thoughts create your emotions and affect your behavior. Thoughts, consisting of a positive nature can lead to desirable consequences. Negative self-talk in large amounts, sets you up for troubles and hardships in the present and future. Learning to think positively is a skill that can be learned by everyone. *Insight, insight, insight* is a must, to prevent you from repeating old, unproductive patterns. Put faith into the words you think and the words you say. Now is the time to take control of your thoughts. Don't put it off. Ask yourself these questions:

- **What words do I say to others?**
- **What words do I say to myself?**
- **Are my words positive or negative?**
- **What changes can I make in my self-talk that would change my behavior in a positive way?**

Always be aware that *you are what you think.* You deserve joy and happiness, and the opportunity to display your gifts and talents. You deserve the choice to celebrate the positive. Here are a few recognizable positive affirmations that you might have heard:

- **"Never Give Up."** — John Cena, WWF champion
- **"Let It Go."** — Sung by Idina Menzel as Elsa in Disney's *Frozen* **and Sylvester Stallone in** *Rambo*
- **"Just Do It"** — Nike
- **"It will all be better tomorrow."** — John Candy in *Uncle Buck*
- **"This is just a test."** — Joel Osteen
- **"Stick to the Plan."** — *Jurassic Park 3*
- **"Stay Focused."** — Pat Morita as Mr. Miyagi in *Karate Kid III*

The great Chinese philosopher Lao Tzu gave us these wonderful words of wisdom:

Watch your thoughts, they become words.
Watch your words, they become actions.
Watch your actions, they become habits.
Watch your habits, they become your character.
Watch your character, it becomes your destiny.

8. Visualization and Relaxation

If you have seen the old Rocky II movie, there is a scene where his corner support is trying to give him confidence between rounds after he is pounded by Apollo Creed. The corner person uses visualization as a way to encourage Rocky to fight on and not give up. While Rocky is in the corner between rounds he is told, "You can't be hurt because you are too tough. He is only a man. You can hurt him because you're a greasy, fast, two-hundred-pound Italian tank." The purpose, of course, is to help Rocky visualize and transform into a fighting machine that is indestructible. Rocky, in turn, goes back into the ring and becomes that tank to take the title from Apollo Creed.

There was a study done by Dr. Biasiotto from the University of Chicago with the hypothesis that the subconscious mind can play a major part in our performance. Basketball players, used in this study, were divided into three groups and their free throw skills were evaluated. The first group practiced their free throws. The second group did not physically practice, but visualized. The third group did not practice or visualize. Results indicated that the players from groups one and two who practiced and visualized, improved significantly. The third group did not. The study lends support to the effectiveness of visualization.

Visualization can be a readily utilized strategy when it comes to anger management. You can visualize yourself standing up to someone, being assertive, and not letting them take advantage of you. Imagine a shield with a suit of armor where hurtful words and negative comments fall helplessly off you. Also possible, is when the visualization is paired with the time-out strategy. Simply imagine taking your time-out in the peacefulness and serenity of a place where you escape from people and events.

Yet another visualization exercise is the use of progressive muscle relaxation paired with visual imagery which involves concentration on specific muscles in order to relax them. This gets rid of the tension that anger produces. It is explained in more detail later in the next exercise.

Relaxation / Visualization Exercise

All right! So far, we have explored eight anger control techniques that are designed to calm us down and react appropriately. In the movie *The War Room,* released in August 2015, the character Elizabeth Jordan is experiencing family problems so she sets up and designs a war room—a specific place free from distractions. She retreats into this room to pray, meditate and be alone. While her family's problems are the main topic, this room turns out to be a place of refuge.

This type of sanctuary can be modified into a place in your house for relaxation and visualization. Once you find a room where you can be alone, you might set the atmosphere. Perhaps a comfortable chair or beanbag might be a good addition, or even just a yoga mat. Pictures could be hung on the wall depicting peaceful scenes such as a tropical beach or a mountain stream. Inspirational quotations could also be included. Once the room is designed, it is ready to put into use. Exercises involve breathing deeply, relaxing various muscle groups in the body, visualizing a place that helps you relax, making you feel at peace. There are many exercises that use progressive muscle relaxation and visualization. Personalizing an exercise for yourself is easy to do. Let's try one.

> Begin by getting comfortable. Relax in your chair or sit on the mat in the yoga Lotus position (legs crossed), just whatever is comfortable for you. Make sure you are free of distractions. Begin to relax by taking some deep breaths. Notice the tension in your face. Contract the muscles and hold for a few seconds. Then let them go. Feel

the difference between when the muscles are relaxed and when they are tense. Next, center your attention on the neck region. Tense the neck muscles and hold for a few seconds. Then let go. Feel the difference between tensed and relaxed muscles. The next area to focus on is the shoulders and back. Tense these muscles and hold for a few seconds. Then let go. Notice the difference between tense and relaxed. The next area of focus is the stomach area. Tighten your stomach and hold for a few seconds. Then let go. Notice the difference between tense and relaxed. Do this same procedure for the buttocks, thighs, calves, and feet. Lie or sit there for a minute or two, enjoying the relaxation before continuing.

Now for the visualization, let us go on a journey to the beach which is a relaxing place for most people. Close your eyes and be very still. What do you hear? Listen for the sounds of the waves in the ocean. Hear them repetitively lapping on the shore. Spend some time here to enjoy peace and serenity.

Notice the breeze from the ocean. You can feel it. You can smell it. You can taste it. What better place is there? Take a deep breath and feel the peace, the calmness. Walk along the shore. Feel the warm sand on the bottom of your feet. You are at a place where peace and serenity are the norm. As you walk, you come across a pair of palm trees. There, in the middle, is a hammock just for you. Lie in it and let the fresh ocean air and the warmth of the sun draw you deeper and deeper into a state of relaxation. Free yourself of the tensions of the day. Feel the heaviness in your face, arms, legs, and feet. You have all the time in the world to relax and enjoy yourself. Make this ocean view your special place where you can go to avoid life's daily tensions. When you are ready, open your eyes, relaxed, refreshed, and ready to continue.

You have just completed a progressive muscle relaxation and visualization exercise. Feel free to make up your own exercises, just as long as they allow you to relax and be ready to meet the stressors of the day with energy and positivity. Remember, you are trying to learn anger control techniques designed especially for you.

9. Take Time Out

He makes me so mad! I'd like to kill him! Did I really think that? *I hope I didn't say that out loud. I must be losing control.* It is definitely time to get away and take a time-out. People become angry and, on occasion, just need to get away for a while. They might walk around the neighborhood or do some yard work. If there is a hiking or bicycle trail nearby, that is a great place to go. The point is to get away from the anger source to calm down. Time out could last anywhere from five minutes to several hours, a day, or longer depending on the severity of the troubling event. Doing physical activities while taking time out like jogging, shooting baskets, exercising, and lifting weights are all considered beneficial because they release energy.

Working with manipulatives (things you control) is another way to take a time-out because it mentally distracts you, allowing you to use the kinesthetic (hands on) modality of learning. Puzzles are a great example of a manipulative. In my work as a grade school principal, *Legos* proved to be invaluable in giving students time to de-escalate and regain their composure. After they calmed down, it became possible to talk about the problem with them. Forcing them to just sitting in time-out is a form of punishment and is not conducive to producing a change in the long run.

Different manipulatives work for different people. Rubik's Cubes, peg games, checkers, and card games are all possibilities. Find out what manipulatives are best for you in advance of your anger episodes. A time-out may be a hobby or something that gives you pleasure like listening to music, working on a car, reading a book, watching a comedy, or playing with your pet. Stay clear of alcohol, drugs, and driving a car while upset. These activities only complicate the problem. Remember, the angrier you get, your thinking processes diminish proportionately. Taking a time-out is an excellent strategy to use. Get away from the source of anger or frustration and find a place or activity that you enjoy. Regain your composure and realign your thinking until you are ready to problem-solve and react appropriately.

10. Be Assertive

Assertiveness is a skill that is learned with practice. There is a fine line between not being passive (letting other people step on your rights), and being aggressive (stepping on the rights of others). To be assertive is to express your opinions, rights, and feelings without showing anger or being upset outwardly. Assertiveness, when acted upon, should exhibit behaviors like good eye contact, speaking clearly and confidently, maintaining serious facial expressions, and good body posture. Assertive people are able to get their point across without demonizing the other person or making them feel bad. Some people refer to assertiveness as "I" statements. An example might be "I think or I would like to say." An "I" statement, delivered in a normal tone of voice, increases your chances of being heard.

It's important to avoid being passive. As with repressed feelings, this stores up a surplus of anger inside you. In fact, passive behavior can encourage others to take advantage of you. Putting other people's needs ahead of your own to **avoid conflict** is a reflection of this behavior pattern. (This is not to be confused with the virtue of humility when you *voluntarily* put others before yourself because of *their* need.) Being passive often leads to resentment and hidden anger. If you're passive, you probably have poor eye contact, talk softly, and have a slouched body posture.

Being aggressive might be the opposite of passive. The essence of aggression is when the aggressor unjustly takes advantage of others with intent to cause harm by means such as bullying, intimidating, or perhaps talking loudly with an attitude, and presuming to always be right. Aggressive people do not care about the rights of others, and are void of empathy and compassion. They might yell, break things, or even become physically abusive to others in extreme cases. This type of person only meets his own needs at the expense of others. The virtue of tolerance is a requirement if you come in contact with someone with this disposition.

Facts to Remember When You Act Assertively

- **Listen carefully for the other person's point of view.**
- **Have control over your temper. Think with your mind, not your emotions.**
- **Be considerate.**
- **Firmness is important. Both individuals have the right to state their feelings and opinions. People don't have the right to expect others to do what they want.**

11. Prayer, Meditation, and Yoga

Prayer is a practice that most Americans and people of religious faiths throughout the world engage in daily. It helps us to remain positive, fights off our depressive tendencies, and gives us the energy to reach out and give service to others. It is a higher form of meditation—a link. This strategy is usually taught in the home or local church. Prayer reduces stress and anger, while increasing capacities for compassion, forgiveness and empathy. The power of prayer cannot be emphasized enough and is a common practice for people of all faiths, all socioeconomic levels, all colors, and all nationalities.

Some people use meditation and yoga as an alternative, or in combination with prayer. There are numerous meditative practices. Meditation reduces stress which contributes to inner peace, resulting in a sense of well-being. Like prayer, it is best to set up a schedule and form a routine.

Yoga, on the other hand, has many similar benefits to meditation. It uses stretching of muscles, meditation, balance and moving your body in differing positions. Just like meditation, it requires regular practice and some form of discipline to a routine schedule. The benefits include increased flexibility and more energy for the events of the day.

12. Find Positive Role Models

Do you remember the advice that many parents and caregivers may have given you while you were growing up? They wanted you to avoid people who were troublemakers and spend more time with those who were respectful and goal-oriented. What they were repeating, in so many words, is what we addressed previously—you take on the characteristics of those you associate with. Role models, in managing anger, are a resource that is often overlooked. To have one positive role model in your life is good. To have several role models is great! Role models should teach you and inspire you through their actions and the qualities they possess. Identify those who are goal-oriented with well-developed values and who practice service to others.

Learning to Problem-Solve

PROBLEM-SOLVING IS OF THE UTMOST IMPORTANCE when it comes to understanding and changing your behavior. As events occur rapidly, your task is to recognize, analyze and react, hopefully in a way that is beneficial for yourself and others. Why? Your choices could have immediate and long-range consequences. These consequences can be either positive or negative. This is why, when left to reactionary impulses, you may make decisions that are not in your best interest. By getting feedback from others, and having a strategy you can refer to, your decisions and reactions may be a great deal more positive.

Following are a **behavior assessment,** and a **role play exercise** that will teach you a valuable technique for problem-solving. Since evaluating your actions is one of the more complex and higher-level thinking skills, it is advisable to complete the exercise with a friend, a family member or even a trained professional such as a counselor or social worker.

The technique described for role play offers detailed procedures, providing the structure to take all the steps you need for the role-playing exercise, and for those events you will encounter in real life. If you feel uncomfortable working with another individual, you can always complete the exercise by yourself. Either way, it is to your benefit to do it. There are many different types of methods you can use for problem-solving. This is just one of many. In case it is awkward to use at first, just remember this process has been used repeatedly with proven results. The more you can use problem-solving techniques successfully, the better consequences you will ensure.

When completing this exercise, remember fundamental rule number five: **"Anger lets us know that there is a problem that needs to be solved."**

Follow these important steps in the process: 1) identify what feeling or feelings occurred before your anger, and 2) determine whether or not these feelings fit the situation.

Processing for Success– Evaluating Your Behavior

To illustrate how the Processing for Success exercise works, see examples in Appendix C.

1. Date happened: _____

2. Where were you when you became angry?
_____

3. What happened? _____

4. Repeat: "I Am Responsible for My Anger and My Feelings."

5. What feelings came before the anger?
_____

6. Did my feelings fit the situation?
Yes _____ No _____

7. What did you do? Prioritize techniques using 1, 2, 3:

___breathed deeply	___counted backward
___Yelled	___talked to an adult
___thought ahead	___talked to a friend
___used profanity	___wrote a letter
___broke something	___positive self-talk
___visualized	___took a time out
___backbiting	___was threatened
___was assertive	___other

8. What self-talk did you use?
_____

9. How did the other person feel?
_____

10. What was the outcome?
_____

11. How angry were you?

___ irritated
___ getting angry
___ angry
___ furious
___ enraged

12. How did you handle the situation?

___ great
___ good
___ okay
___ not so well
___ poorly

13. What is your plan for success in the future?
_____

14. Repeat: "I will remain positive and not focus on the negative."

Role Play

ROLE PLAY IS AN ART FORM THAT ALLOWS you to act out your feelings and emotions through body movement and expressive statements. It can be a great way to see and practice your behavior. If you are serious about making changes in the way you respond to others when your emotions get high, this technique is one of the best. It requires you to analyze your anger and the stress-provoking situation, create a plan for future encounters and then evaluate success in meeting your goal.

Be familiar with and practice role playing. Understand it, apply it, and put it to good use. Program yourself for success. This strategy can provide insight to help you with self-control and communication skills in the future.

Procedure: Three or more people are needed to perform the role play, and will trade parts until everyone has had a turn. The main character is the one who practices using short-term anger reducers. A second person (could actually be two or more individuals) is selected to be the anger trigger. A third person acts as the facilitator. The main character must create a plan he will follow

the next time his anger trigger occurs. Once they practice the plan, the main character is required to evaluate the performance to see if he could follow this same procedure when the trigger happens again to him. (An example will follow.)

First, write the letters A C T S on a paper or tablet.

- A = the anger trigger
- C = the character(s) involved in the situation
- T = the techniques to be practiced
- S = the setting

The participants practice two to three anger control techniques for each situation. Each person needs to put the techniques in the order she/he would use them. For example: "First, I will take a deep breath. Next, I will do positive self-talk. Finally, I will take a time-out." It is important to be very specific. If the main character chooses self-talk, what specifically will the person say to him/herself? If the person is going to take a time-out, where is he going to do that and what will he do? The first time the individual engages in negative thinking or actions, the role play is terminated and the participants are encouraged to try again with a more positive approach. Here is an example of a plan:

Role Play for Anger

(It is helpful to write out the script on something erasable.)

A – Tom is teasing Mary. Tom is the anger trigger.

C – Mary is the victim who will practice the anger control techniques. Sasha, a friend, will be the facilitator.

T – Mary chooses to take a deep breath. Next, she will use the following self-talk: "Just ignore him and walk away. He is not worth getting upset over." Finally, she will take a time-out and go for a walk after school.

S – Middle School lunch hour.

When you are involved in doing role plays, always concentrate on the positive and downplay the negative. When you find yourself breaking away from the script you created, the facilitator should instruct you to stop. Once you have stopped, start over from the beginning, practicing until you are able to perform it positively and successfully.

When using self-talk in your role play, say it out loud so you can get used to saying it. When you actually use self-talk in a real-life situation, you say it to yourself and not voice it so anyone else can hear. After you have successfully completed the role play, you should sit down with the people you are working with and have a discussion, each giving feedback on the performance completed. Video-taping the role-play on your phone or with a camcorder is very helpful. This can help you form a "mental picture" of how to perform and what to improve.

Beware of Escalating Anger

AGGRESSIVE BEHAVIOR IS A STRATEGY OR WAY FOR some people to cope with their underlying, uncomfortable, and painful feelings when they don't know what else to do. They simply lack insight and training. They are different from the small number of people who display this behavior because they simply choose not to care and are mean, hateful, and antisocial for other reasons. But for those who feel like they have been backed against a wall with no way out, there are interventions that can be implemented at any time as long as the person is not out of control. Caution should always be observed because some interventions can escalate the situation. Certain words can even be a trigger. Some examples follow.

Audrey has just entered the classroom. Over the last month, the teacher has noticed that Audrey has become increasingly defiant and negative. She has disrupted the class on several occasions. The teacher, trying to decide how to handle the situation, is getting more upset and having less patience. "Audrey, **you** need to get over here right now. We are in a classroom where there are people trying to learn. **You should** know how to act. **You** have so much potential, **but** you'll **never** succeed with that attitude. **You** should **always** show self-control if you expect to be successful. I just **can't** let you get by in this class with that type of attitude."

The boldface words in the preceding paragraph are triggers that maintain or escalate anger. The more the teacher uses them, the more angry Audrey will become. Here is why: The word "should" does not allow Audrey to have any control. A person who is angry or becoming angry needs to be allowed more room for control if she is to calm down. The word *but* tends to trigger a negative response. The word you casts blame on Audrey directly. The word can't takes away options. Angry people need options to prevent their anger from increasing. Always and never also are words that provide an angry person with no options. Instead, it is preferable for the teacher to make an "I statement" which shows ownership of her comments so that Audrey's anger is reduced, not increased. "I feel frustrated because both of us seem to have difficulty in communicating with each other. I would like to improve on that. Do you have any ideas?"

When You Encounter an Angry Person

FIRST, DON'T GET ANGRY YOURSELF! YOU MUST portray a caring attitude toward the person. Sometimes this can be very difficult, almost impossible in extreme cases. You don't have to be perfect with some of the following steps as long you stay focused with the right attitude. First, you might ask the person, "Are you all right?" and sincerely mean it. This demonstrates that you genuinely care about her feelings. Next, it is important just to listen. That sounds simple enough, but might be difficult to do. Since the person is in pain, she needs to verbally express the feelings or thoughts she is experiencing, which might be difficult to hear or not judge. If you are well acquainted with the individual, remind her of how well she has done in past situations. Take time to emphasize the positives, her strengths. Whatever you do, avoid coming up with solutions for the person. This only makes the problem worse and can backfire on you. Examples of what you might say are: "You have always been tolerant of other people. That is one of your gifts." "You are amazing when it comes to being fair."

Keeping Your Cool When Someone is Angry at You

THE WHOLE SITUATION IS DIFFERENT WHEN THERE IS someone angry at you. Your options are limited. When the person begins letting his anger out, all you can do is to relax and perhaps take a deep breath. Remain as calm as possible. The person has to let his feelings out so you need to remain as silent as you can. This is the most difficult part. If you can do this, the rest is easy. Once again, you tell yourself to remain calm and take another deep breath. Reasoning and problem solving can only be done when the one who is angry regains composure. Arrange a time with the person to later talk about the problem. That's it. Simple to think about. Difficult to execute.

What have we learned about angry people? They are in pain! We have also discovered it is difficult to reason with them. Their negative feelings are controlling their actions. As they become angrier and angrier, they are no longer able to think clearly. All you can do is to keep your talking to a minimum and listen to what they have to say. It is their responsibility, not yours, in choosing whether to react positively or negatively.

Chapter 4: The World Of Feelings And How We Deal With Them

Dealing With Painful & Uncomfortable Feelings

Why is it so important to understand and identify feelings? Because feelings are often expressed through anger. Unless you know its source, you can't understand where your anger comes from and, most importantly, the best way to get rid of it permanently. Think about a wound with a scab. The scab is anger, but your wound won't heal because there is an infection (underlying feeling) that is making it worse. You have to treat the infection before the scab drops off to restore the skin to what it should be.

What Is Repression?

Sometimes when life becomes too painful, you have to do something to get relief. As your brain searches for a way to cope, an option is to use the defense mechanism known as repression. Magically, it automatically blocks out feelings from your memory. It is designed to protect your daily thoughts from buried, painful, stressful emotions. Memories of past events are erased from your conscious mind, allowing you to go about your daily routines as if they never occurred. On the surface, you might be energetic, happy and possibly enthusiastic, but underneath trouble is lurking. The longer you fail to acknowledge the hidden, buried emotions, a storm begins to form. As time goes on, without intervention, much damage can take place. This is one of the most harmful ways in which we might deal with painful and uncomfortable feelings. It is also one of the most damaging because we don't even realize those repressed feelings exist. We only are aware of the symptoms they cause when they manifest as unexplained mental or physical issues.

What Is Suppression?

Suppression is another way we handle painful and uncomfortable feelings. When we suppress something that has happened, we do it *on purpose* in order to handle multiple problems at the same time. This can be useful. For example, you have a big fight with your parents. You are extremely upset, but you go to school and try to have a normal day. You socialize with your friends. You concentrate on your schoolwork and take an important chapter test in one of your classes. After school, you learn new plays on the football field or routines as a cheerleader. While your day progresses, you forget all about the fight you had with your parents. You do this on purpose so you can make it through the day. Later, when you get home, you remember the fight and can deal with the difficulties. Suppression simply blocks out feelings intentionally and is done in the short term to handle problems.

Repression vs. Suppression (Differences and Coping)

It is not uncommon to confuse repression with suppression. Repression is very difficult to recognize and deal with. As noted earlier, clues to its existence may manifest in physical and mental issues, but they can also show up through disturbed interpersonal relationships, poor self-esteem, prolonged feelings of hopelessness, and extremes in negative feelings.

Since the person is unaware of what is going on, it may be required to consult a counselor, social worker or mental health professional who is trained to discover some of the symptoms of this complex process, and to make sure the individual receives the right professional help.

Since repression comes from our unconscious mind, one situation where you might suppress memories is if you experienced abuse in your childhood. The shame and guilt is overwhelming, much too difficult to even try to handle. Whether the experience was physical or sexual abuse, you were innocent and did not know what was happening. All you knew then was that something was wrong. Maybe you even thought it was your fault. Now you are in your teenage years and you have to carry around that baggage.

Repression might also perhaps occur if, for example, your mother died last year. You went to the funeral and kept your emotions inside of you. It definitely hurt, but you went on and made the best of it. You did not go through the grieving stage which is normal for people who have lost a loved one. There is an emptiness, but you fight it off. You cope by carrying on as usual.

Maybe at school, one of the players on the football team is always harassing you. Unfortunately, you share a locker with him. Every time he has the locker open, upon your arrival, he slams it shut. At lunchtime, he makes a scene in taunting you so everyone in the cafeteria can see. When school ends, you try to slip out without him seeing you. This makes your life miserable. You would rather stay at home than endure another day at school. You feel humiliated, degraded, defeated. The next year, you become a senior and he has graduated. What a relief, but the feelings that accumulated from the previous year continue to remain trapped. They are still there because you have not brought them to a conscious level. You are shy, timid, unsure of yourself. This affects your relationships with others.

As mentioned earlier, repression can be harmful to your physical and emotional well-being. Ignoring your feelings, whether it be for <u>several</u> months or years, can lead you down the road to trouble and hardships. There is extensive research that indicates repression is related to high blood pressure, heart problems, eating disorders, ulcers, headaches, rashes, and even cancer, also leaving you vulnerable to colds and other illnesses. This is such a common result of unresolved feelings, you will see physical reactions mentioned throughout this book. In some cases, it can even lead to depression as well as negatively influence your current feelings and thoughts. Highly unusual, <u>but</u> a person could even suffer from amnesia.

What course of action do you take to avoid the destructive forces of repression? The first step is to become aware that it exists. For repression resulting from childhood abuse, there is only one course of action—professional help. You may be hesitant to seek it, but it is something you really need. If you don't, you may have many failed relationships in your life. There are probably many other events that are currently in your life where you may have used the defense mechanism of repression. I know I have mentioned this often, but it does help talk to a friend or adult who is capable of empathy.

Repression traps a great deal of energy within you that is not being released. This is where the many available sports at school can become valuable. Just pick one or more. Let that stored-up energy out in a productive way. Mentally, you can release it through the arts such as painting, music, or photography. Another helpful option is during prayer or meditation when you can take time for self-reflection in a place of safety and solitude. In a state of deep relaxation, go back and relive situations in your life that were painful and disturbing. Try to remember the setting, identify the feelings, and analyze your reactions. Once you have identified and confronted feelings of the past, be optimistic, positive, and take charge. Be confident and assertive. Make your life better by accepting positive and negative feelings, knowing that they are both a part of being human. Make your needs known to others, but realize that they have needs of their own. You now have conquered some of the ghosts of your past and can move on, giving yourself a fresh start.

Feelings occur to us frequently and are constantly changing as each day, sometimes hours, go by. Some are pleasant and some are not. They bring you up and they bring you down. They are a natural part of our psychological makeup. Who doesn't like the pleasant ones such as joy, happiness, excitement, and love? Unpleasant feelings are a different story. No matter how hard you try to avoid them, there they are, continuing to crop up, testing your limits. Embarrassment, loneliness, and hurt, to name a few, attack your spirit to cause you pain and discomfort. Then there is grief, in a category by itself—the feeling that everyone would like to avoid. Unbearable sorrow, and heartbreak beyond compare, consume your innermost being. Grief is the villain whenever death is the culprit that steals a loved one.

No one can ever be free of the clutches of this complexity of feelings. When it comes to feelings, you can soar in the heavens or struggle for survival. By creating the physical, intellectual, emotional, and spiritual dimensions, the Creator has provided you with the tools to progress in this world and the next. Feelings, in particular, are instruments you use, along with others, to handle hardships and withstand difficulties. They allow you to grow, develop virtues, and build character. Anger, as explored earlier in-depth, is one of those emotions that must be kept under control in order for all of the other feelings to be expressed.

You can, however, become a prisoner of your feelings. Getting up in the morning with the sun shining through the window, you feel positive energy flow through your body. Things are good when you leave the house. What a wonderful day it is until something or someone upsets you. Your mood changes almost instantaneously and the day quickly deteriorates. Basically, you let your emotions take control and they determine what kind of day you are going to have. One thing we do know, you can't always control your thoughts and feelings, but you can control your reactions.

People are more comfortable with talking about and sharing pleasurable feelings. But avoidance is a natural choice when exploring painful feelings. Be honest. They make you feel bad and can put you in a foul mood. They hurt, so why bother talking about them? Making a choice of how you are going to respond to undesirable feelings is within your control. Both healthy and unhealthy behavioral responses exist. Strategies of reflection and assertiveness are healthy choices when you are hurt by someone. Tell them how you feel and stand up for yourself. A significant loss, like the death of someone close, end of a friendship, death of a pet, or the loss of personal property may be too overwhelming and painful, initially resulting in an extended period before action is taken.

One method that has been advocated by research in managing uncomfortable feelings is to change your thinking pattern. Cognitive behavioral therapies, in recent years, have been used to teach individuals how to change their thoughts, which then has an effect of changing their feelings and actions. Restructuring how you think about a life problem is a powerful strategy. Unfortunately, it can be difficult to put into action and requires effort and training. Controlling our thoughts is not easy. Everyone knows that from personal experience.

In our society, we fail to do a very good job when it comes to teaching individuals the importance of feelings and being able to identify them. If feelings are so important and can cause numerous physical ailments, why isn't there more of an effort to teach them to our children, youth, and adults? That is a good question and one of the reasons for this book.

Depression

Weeks go by and you don't have any energy. It's hard to get up in the morning for school. Your self-esteem plummets. Feelings of worthlessness consume your mind as you try to just get through each day. Life doesn't seem to be worth living. Hopelessness sets in. If all of these symptoms are occurring within you, there is a good chance that you are beginning to enter the throes of depression.

Where does depression come from? Is it possible to prevent it? When painful feelings are left inside you, without attention, they become stronger as time goes on. Past events, weaving into feelings can sabotage your view of the world and your place in it. These distortions could evolve into physical attacks on your body, and depression could become a realization. Then too, if anger lurks just below the surface over an extended period, regardless of whether it is outwardly or inwardly directed, it can lead to depression, unhappiness, and less stability.

Reverting back to your childhood, if abuse of any kind was the norm, it could be a stimulus for your current depression. This, in turn, could negatively influence future and romantic relationships. Anger disguises your underlying feelings. What kinds of behavior might you see as a result? This change might surface in you as extreme nervousness, fear of attempting something new, or isolating yourself from your friends and activities that you once enjoyed. But past abuse is only one of many possible events leading to the road of depression. Current abuse as being constantly bullied is another circumstance. Each day, getting up in the morning, knowing that a student or number of students will torment you, makes your life miserable. You can only take this form of abuse so long before succumbing to its pressure.

Many ill effects can result while in the depths of depression. The feeling of hopelessness is the most obvious. There is no desire to do or accomplish anything. Each day is a challenge to make it through another futile routine. Caution needs to be exercised during this time since you become prone to engage in dangerous habits and urges. Eating disorders, along with physical issues such as headaches and ulcers could crop up. Addictions and isolation are more likely to occur in this mental state. But when a person deteriorates in the entanglement of depression, he contemplates the worst possible solution—the consideration of suicide. The National Suicide Prevention Lifeline is 988.

If you are experiencing depression, it is best to push yourself in maintaining your daily routine. You may not feel motivated and get no enjoyment of doing so, but it is best to continue with as much normalcy as possible. This relieves your mind from obsessing over the negative and provides a source of energy that can be used for productivity. If you feel like isolating yourself, make sure your best friend or someone close to you is there to help you through this rough time. Activities such as volunteering at a charitable organization and giving assistance to the elderly allow your attention to be focused on others, and makes you forget your own needs.

Visualization of a happier or more pleasant experience and setting might also give you some relief. Saying positive affirmations quietly or out loud to yourself each morning is another beneficial activity. For instance, "I will do my best today to help others and be happy." "I will try my best in my classes and stay in contact with my friends." "I can do this..." As said repeatedly in this book, over and over and over, one of the most effective interventions is to talk to a friend or adult. Do not let your inner thoughts get the best of you.

If none of the aforementioned activities help you to move out of your depression, the final stage of intervention is to be referred to a mental health worker, where therapy and medications might be used on a temporary basis.

Shame and Guilt

Two emotions, which are in a category of their own, are the twin evils of destruction—shame and guilt. They prevent you from forgiving yourself and cause self-degradation. In her book *Overcoming Toxic Emotions,* Leah Guy describes these feelings as "Guilt says, 'You did something wrong,' while shame says, 'Something is wrong with you.'" Feeling like viruses, they often date back in history from dysfunctional families or a troubled past. They are buried deep into your unconscious mind. You are totally oblivious to their existence. Past events allow them to grow, intertwining with other feelings, sabotaging your view of the world and you in it. Repressed and distorted, they attack your self-esteem and hinder you from achieving your goals. Relationships are weakened, and interpersonal interactions distorted. They are the springboard that lay the groundwork for entanglement of other negative emotions.

Similar to guilt, shame also has its roots in the past. If a child is constantly criticized, yelled at, ignored, physically or sexually abused, they might store up feelings of shame. Because of their innocence, they believe, for example, that it is their fault for their parents' behavior towards them. Perhaps, if they weren't so bad, their parents wouldn't have acted the way they did towards them.

Perhaps even now, current situations are causing you shame as in the following scenarios.

SCENARIO ONE:

You're a student in middle school and you are struggling in your language arts class.

The teacher is always on your case. You are lucky if you get a "D" on an assignment.

The grades are posted each week for everyone in the school to see. The teacher has had numerous conferences with your parents. You feel worthless. It is all your fault. You say to yourself, "I am stupid. I am dumb. There is something wrong with me." Shame has made a claim on you.

SCENARIO TWO:

You had to do it. There was a foreign exchange student who transferred from Spain. Wow! She was very pretty with a great personality. The dilemma, which you find yourself in, is that you are in a long-term and committed relationship with your girlfriend who is in her first year of college. You plan to join her next year when you graduate from high school.

Unfortunately, you are lonely so you ask the new girl on several dates, enjoying her company. Then, your girlfriend comes home for a visit. She tells you how much she loves you. Your guilt runs high because you did something wrong by breaking your promise to be faithful. How are you going to correct the problem or are you even going to try?

Unlike shame, guilt does have a positive dimension. We can always make up for or learn from the wrong we committed.

It is common to erect your shield of repression to protect yourself, to avoid these two destructive emotions. Our guilt and shame are washed away, at least until we lower the shield.

Unfortunately, a long-term cover-up of these feelings distorts our relationships and is detrimental to our health and happiness. As long as the shield is up, we don't have to feel that we are "bad" people. We don't have to feel that we are responsible for all of the mistakes we have made.

Unknowingly and unintentionally people in our environment spread the seeds of shame and guilt, even though this is not their intent. For example, when parents are too strict and go to extremes in correcting the misbehavior of their children, they could spread these two emotions. Teachers in our schools, who are strict and harshly correct their students on their performance, are also spreaders of these toxic emotions. Even in churches, priests and ministers in their sermons may instill a dose of shame and guilt in the congregation if their messages are too strong. The right amount of teaching and lecturing is good, so long as it is not done in excess.

Shame and guilt are tough feelings to deal with. They have been the downfall of many people, but there is something that you can do about them. The first step is awareness. This could be accomplished through prayer and meditation. Once this step is taken, positive affirmations can be employed. For shame, examples include: "It's not my fault." "I know it's not true." "I am a good person." For guilt, it is best to release and pardon yourself with declarations such as: "I will make amends." "I will correct my mistakes." "I will not do it again." Shame and guilt are destructive forces, definitely some of the most difficult of all the emotions to confront, especially shame. Professional assistance should probably be sought to make effective changes if these feelings originated from your childhood.

Grief

Grief is in a league all by itself. This is a nasty emotion that is complex and consists of many feelings wrapped into one. Perhaps the most painful of all emotions, it is an exception to the rule that feelings are temporary. What sets it apart from all of the other emotions is that the pain never goes away as in when a loved one dies. You just find various ways to cope as time passes because there is no greater agony that you must endure. Grief is a form of separation anxiety in its highest form, and unfortunately, it is natural and common to us all. And as difficult as it is to experience it, grief does help to strengthen our character and prepare us spiritually.

In coping with this feeling, it is important to acknowledge there are different levels and reasons for grieving. All losses are considerably less intense than the death of a loved one, yet it is necessary to acknowledge and grieve them. Examples are the loss of a pet (for some, this is like a family member), job termination, or losing a house because of a disaster (fire, tornado, etc.). Loss is the key focus—you lose something that you love or has value to you in this world, and you can't get it or them back. You are powerless. It is not in your control. Feeling grief once is bad enough, but you have to continually experience and endure it many times throughout your lifetime. This is one of the great sufferings in this plane of your existence. No one can alter it; preparing for it is almost impossible. So, what is the plan? How do you deal with it? In one way, you, as being part of the younger generation, are lucky. You do not have to experience the same number of deaths that an adult has to cope with because of your age, but as you get older, you will have more such occurrences too.

Mourning the loss of a loved one can play tricks on your mind and body. The loss of self-control, nightmares as you sleep, and the pain fading in and out causes you emotional upheaval and exhaustion. Headaches are more frequent, loss of energy is at its highest, and the digestive system is out of whack. You are vulnerable. You yearn for relief. It is at this moment that relief might lead you to some type of addiction. Beware of alcohol consumption, marijuana use, drugs, and promiscuity. Be alert for the early signs of depression. It is normal for this feeling to occur in some form after such a major a loss. Now, for the most serious reaction to death, your mind creates thoughts of possible suicide. If this occurs, don't wait to get help. This has been mentioned before because it is so critical. The loss of a loved one is overwhelming.

Grief can definitely affect your performance at school. You can be on the honor roll and still have trouble with your grades. It becomes increasingly hard to focus on any goal-directed activities. Motivation can deteriorate. Sometimes you find yourself just going through the motions. Socially, there can be a change as well. Interest in activities may decline. Obsessing over the loss during class by daydreaming does not help your situation. You're irritable. People tend to avoid you. When things don't go your way, you can go into a state of anger quickly. Let's face it, you are sad and that is perfectly normal. The anger you are experiencing is a symptom of how you are coping with the sadness. You will not always respond this way, and eventually you will find other ways to manage your grief.

A pioneer in the field of grief, Elizabeth Kubler Ross, is a psychiatrist and medical doctor who interviewed more than 200 patients who were dying. She conducted one of the most famous psychological studies of the late twentieth century. The results are referred to as "The five stages of grief." As we briefly go through them, please realize that this is just a theory. Some people might not go through all of the stages and the order that is presented, but it acts as a guide, and the best one that we have to date.

The Five Stages of Grief

Stage one is the feeling of isolation. You can't believe it happened and are in shock. It hits you out of nowhere and is so painful to imagine that you hide it in the back of your mind. You think to yourself, *this really didn't happen.* You refuse to accept it. The pain is so great, you take measures to protect yourself through denial. You buy some time to acclimate to the pain.

In **stage two** anger, rage, resentment all come to the surface because they cover up the underlying hurtful and painful feelings to protect you. As Dr. Kubler-Ross puts it, "Why me?" Anger allows you to manage the pain so that it doesn't overwhelm you. You fade in and out of anger and the deep-seated feelings associated with grief. You need to find ways to distract yourself as you go through this difficult time.

Stage three is bargaining. This is where a person examines his actions. What could he have done to prevent the loss? You promise to *never* or *always* in an attempt to control the pain and fear of loss.

Stage four is depression. The anger and resentment turn inward because of so great a loss. This is where your feelings become intense and you go through the process of mourning. It's natural to feel sadness and to fear the unknown, but it is still difficult. The loss of a spouse, a parent, or a child challenges you to the greatest degree of your existence. The evolving emotions of grieving continue to come in waves as the days and months go by. Remember, the grieving process takes time and you have to go through it at your own pace. All of what you have gone through is part of the healing process.

Stage five is acceptance. This is where we resolve the conflict, one that is spiritual in nature, but beware. Don't get stuck in the grieving process. Let it flow through you the way it is supposed to do. Blocking or ignoring it sets you up for some complicated problems. Remember, you never get over the pain when a loved one passes on to the next world. The pain only lessens with time.

The American television personality, Doctor Oz, aired a television show where his guests were grieving women who had lost their sons to violence. The pain that these mothers had gone through, and continue to go through, is gut-wrenching. To lose one of your children has to be one of the most overwhelming, painful losses that a parent could go through in life. You could hear the pain and anger in their voices as they described the events surrounding their sons' deaths.

Finding outlets for your pain after a loss is very important. Sometimes you just need to let out a good cry. Spending quality time with your friends helps you realize you are not alone. Stay busy with hobbies: listening to music, reading, writing, exercising, art, whatever gives you enjoyment. Look through old photographs, listen to the songs your loved one enjoyed, pray for them, visit their grave site. Frame their picture and hang it on the wall where you can see it most often. Wear a necklace or a piece of their jewelry to remind you of him or her. Don't make any big decisions right away. Set small goals to work towards. Take time to heal. As stated previously, grief is a common occurrence in life and the grieving process is part of the human condition.

Sadness

This emotion can be recognized by tracing it to a specific cause, usually centering on some type of loss. Ending a relationship, a fight with your friend, moving to a new school, and getting a ticket for speeding are examples. Failure to succeed with something can also result in sadness such as poor grades and being fired from a job as well as having a physical injury or illness. This emotion, unlike others, is easy to recognize and most people realize when they are sad. This feeling lets you know you are in some type of pain. It seems to be the opposite of happy. But, in actuality, there are different levels of sadness, and different intensities. Sadness is on the lower end; a higher level is misery. Yet, another is sorrow. This feeling occurs often in some people, more than others, and is quite normal.

When you are sad, you often require some nurturing from another person to help lift your spirit. Finding the right person to give you the nurturing may require some searching, but from past experience, you know who can help you feel better and who will not. You can also engage in something that will express your feelings—write poetry, draw, listen to music, meditate, pray, or do self-reflection. Exercise, go for a walk, or do some type of physical activity. Recognize this feeling of sadness will pass and that it is one of those feelings that should be brief. You can be sad today, and tomorrow you feel fine. It is going to be okay, so try to make it through the day. Teenagers, in particular, experience more emotional highs and lows than any other age group.

If you cannot shake off your sadness and it becomes prolonged, you need to eliminate it and turn things around. Why is this important? First of all, it doesn't feel good, and no one wants to be sad. The joy of living is stifled. If left unchecked, it could lead to far greater problems with your physical well-being and make you tired with little or no energy. Positive thoughts will vacate your mind and be replaced with negative ones, and hopelessness may temporarily find a home in your mind. Do not let sadness linger on. You may need more extensive support to help you than required with temporary sadness.

Failure

You can make it positive or you can make it negative. Failure means not succeeding at some task or behavior that you are trying to perform or complete. You have an expectation in your mind that you will be good at basketball. When you get on the court, you can't even make simple shots. "What? I flunked my American Government class! You got to be kidding. That means I have to take it again next semester."

In school, there are students with many different learning styles. For those who do not conform to the normal methods of learning, the school system puts labels on them like learning disabled, dyslexia, attention deficit disorder, and hyperactivity. Students with these types of labels, even though many are of average to above average intelligence, often struggle, coming up against failure on a regular basis. Failure is real, but it is often a precursor to success.

When you're a teenager, small failures seem to be big and overwhelming. As an adult, you will discover that you will have many failures and you get used to them as being a normal part of life. However, failure, if left unchecked, can lead to some undesirable behaviors. Feelings of worthlessness and inadequacy are the immediate concerns. Not passing your classes is a major dilemma in regard to failure. Alcohol consumption, drug abuse, casual sex, and possible pregnancy increases in probability if enough failure is accumulated. Somewhere, sometime you have to learn that failure is normal and you might need extra help. But first, determine if you are reacting to failure in a healthy or unhealthy manner. Are you unmotivated and feeling a loss of energy? How about your academic performance? Good or not good? If not good, are you faking illness to avoid school or being truant? What about trying new things? Are you resistant? If you answered yes to any of these questions, chances that you are reacting to failure in an unhealthy manner.

You need to find some solutions to get back on the right path. There is one way to deal a blow to failure. Get your courage back and try again. Refuse to give up. Practice the skill you are trying to learn with time and effort. What else? Seek help from a friend or an adult, of course. There is no shame in this. With a friend, you can share your feelings and get reassurance. With an adult, you can get advice on how to solve the problem. Reach out. You may also want to write down and keep the following quote by Oliver Goldsmith, a noted 18th century Irish author, playwright, and poet as an encouraging reminder whenever you experience failure: "Success consists of getting up just one more time than you fall."

Harmful Thoughts (Suicidal, Hurting Yourself or Others, Hurting Animals, Destroying Property)

Harmful thoughts are nothing more than hatred toward oneself. It doesn't get any worse than this. You might show other people mercy, but for you there is none. Forgiveness of self is out of the question. You are entrenched in negative self-talk and the more you do it, the worse your self-esteem. Your thoughts become repetitive, with their motive being to punish yourself. Where does this evil come from? Why do you have to feel this way?

As previously discussed, the severity of these behaviors is often the result of buried, painful feelings such as shame and guilt. If, for example, you were abused during your childhood, there is a good chance you have repressed the cause and these feelings are the result of not being resolved. It doesn't have to originate in your childhood, but you can be sure that there are disturbing, underlying feelings that are buried deep in your unconscious mind.

Realize that your life may be at stake if no action is taken. Your attention needs to be immediate! Self-hatred may lead you to find ways to hurt your body or end your life. Your death could affect the people you love or who love you with a pain they might have to endure for the rest of their lives. But if your intent is to punish others in this way, you will miss the opportunity to show them just how valuable you are. And if your self-hatred causes you to (or want to) harm or punish others, including poor defenseless animals, please seek help immediately. When you are a danger to yourself, others and all living things, you have a problem, and then we all have a problem. There are suicide hotlines and caring mental health professionals who are trained to help you when those thoughts arise. Medication and therapy are often used to get you back on the right track so you can lead a happy and enjoyable life.

Dependency

What does the feeling of dependency mean? Dependency is a learned behavior and is usually associated with a lack of confidence. You believe that other people's needs are more important than your own. You display passive behavior. Because your self-esteem is so low, you are easily influenced. You rely on another person to feel good about yourself.

Addiction is an outgrowth of dependency, whether it be to alcohol, drugs, sex, overeating, or over-working. While all are harmful, please take special note that the most common of these addictions is to drugs and alcohol. Both are damaging to your mind and body. You might be tempted to use them to take the edge off of the pain you feel, or as a way to defer coping with a situation. In both cases, you are trying *not* to feel. But besides causing long term physical damage such as cirrhosis of the liver as with alcohol abuse, it prevents you from being able to resolve whatever you are trying to avoid. You might also miss out on the ability to mature with your peers. If you prevent learning how to cope with your problems today, you will be delayed in knowing how to cope with some important ones you will encounter as a responsible adult. If that happens, you might find that others think you are immature for your age because you will be.

Under-developed social skills make you an easy target for members of the wrong crowd. They can lead you to places where you do not want to be because you are easily swayed. They take pleasure in drinking and doing drugs. But they are nice to you. You feel a sense of belonging while around them. You no longer have to feel alone or isolated. You have a circle of friends to be with, to socialize with and share common interests. Beware, you take on characteristics of the people you associate with.

Scenario One:

You are in your freshman year of high school. You are shy and have trouble socializing. You are introduced to another girl. You enjoy spending time with her, but you continue to be shy around other students. If she goes to a school event, you have to go with her to feel comfortable in that setting. She likes you but gets somewhat irritated with your need to be around her so much. In the meantime

you, because of your dependency on her, are missing out on school activities that you might enjoy—making new friends, attending sporting events, going to parties. You need the security of that special person. If she has her own interests, you spend more time at home. You are wasting away your high school years.

While the above scenario doesn't indicate the influence of a bad character, the "needy" dependence upon another person is not healthy. There must be a way to combat dependency and free yourself from this sort of isolation. The first and most important rule is to stay away from the wrong crowd. Being influenced by an individual who is always getting in trouble, or who is involved in conflicts with others, is a path that you do not want to follow. Instead, join school clubs and activities. These are great places to meet new people and establish friends. Working with other students and sharing a common interest increases your circle of friends and improves your social skills. Participating in sports, especially team sports, builds strong bonds between players. Each player depends on the other for the success of their team. This bond goes beyond the team and beyond the school.

Victimization

Victimization occurs far too often in our society. For some reason, a person or a group of people are targeted unjustly for some reason. Often it is outright prejudice as a result of race, religion, gender, ethnicity, or sexual orientation. These attacks, both verbally and physically, are the result of some insecurity on the part of the person or group of people doing the unfair treatment. The targeted victim feels, as a result, unsafe because victimization instills stress and fear into people's lives.

He is a geek. Everyone knows it at school. It's obvious. For some reason, geeks are easy targets for the students who are insecure and want to maintain a tough image at school. The bully criticizes, makes fun of, and pushes around the weaker students who may be very smart, but physically inferior. The bully enjoys it just because he can. Then there is the gay guy. He receives a lot of abuse and isolation at school. In the cafeteria, no one will sit with him; he has to eat alone. Then there are racial groups like African-Americans who are often targeted and hassled more than their white counterparts. They have endured discrimination within our society for years, some even denied access to basic human rights. The Jewish community has also been a group long targeted by anti-Semites, and we see a growing number of other cultures and ethnicities become victims of attacks described as "hate" crimes.

What can you do if you are being victimized at school? You need to find confidence in yourself and your beliefs. You need to stand up to the bully and tell him how you feel. It's important not to back down and not give in, and that is hard to do. Find a group of friends who are supportive and accepting. Establish relationships. Another intervention, as noted repeatedly, is to talk to an adult such as your parent, a teacher, a coach, or a counselor. Just don't ignore the situation and your feelings.

Visualization Exercise: the Ocean

Let's zero in on our visualization skills again to get a better understanding of how anger and undesirable feelings mix together as they work inside of you.

Visualization is an effective technique to manage feelings—use your imagination as you take an in-depth lesson in identifying your feelings.

Get comfortable. Take some deep breaths. Make sure you are relaxed.

We'll start with our familiar scene of an ocean that we earlier visualized for one of the anger management technique exercises. First, recall your vision if you have ever been to the beach and witnessed or seen videos of a body of water the size of an ocean. *Amazing, breathtaking,* and *awe-inspiring* are adjectives that describe this beautiful view. You look out as far as you can see. The water seems endless. Listen carefully and you can hear the countless waves rolling in rhythm onto the shore.

The Atlantic and Pacific are two of the major oceans that most of us are familiar with, but ponder for a moment to visualize another type of ocean, one consisting of nothing but feelings. This ocean is so vast that it is difficult to comprehend, going beyond the horizon, farther than any eye can see. Upon observation of this ocean, like other oceans, it is rarely calm. You see small waves washing to the shore in a definite rhythm with a steady beat, calming the nerves, and mesmerizing. Now imagine that these smaller waves represent mild emotions like irritation, embarrassment and disappointment, all of which we can handle daily with few, if any, problems.

Then there are the bigger waves that come crashing onto the beaches with a mighty force. Surfers love these waves. What a thrill to ride them, control and conquer them! Sometimes they wipe out and other times they ride them to the shore, relishing their accomplishments. These waves represent greater challenges, feelings of being controlled, feelings of suspicion, feelings of being ignored or used, as well as frustration, rejection, depression. They can be handled on the spot, but may require a time-out and self-reflection.

Get on a boat and venture out further into the ocean. Suddenly, a violent storm erupts, tossing the boat to and fro, waves splashing on the deck. Panic sets in as control of the boat becomes less and less possible. When this happens, it is too late to gain control. Your anger goes to the level of rage. Your speech and actions are then programmed to either hurt others or yourself. Feelings such as being trapped, humiliated, lost, abandoned, crushed, defeated, and betrayed consume you. The ocean is penetrating the heart of your soul. The pain is intense and negative consequences await you. It has now become crucial to identify these feelings, analyze the situations causing them, decide your course of action, and carry it out. Suppression, as an alternative, could lead to crippling outcomes.

Feelings: How To Identify

OUR NEXT SECTION WILL TAKE US TO the heart of this book—how to identify your feelings in various situations and rank them according to their level of severity. For many of you, this will be your first formal training in the identification and acceptance of the feelings that you experience frequently, even daily. This learning process takes time and effort to master, but it is so important that you put your effort into this lesson. Before you can identify feelings, you need to establish a feeling vocabulary and be able to pair each word with its definition. If you are unfamiliar with some of the words, there are various ways in which you can learn the definitions of those used in this program. The first way, of course, is just to study and memorize them. Refer to the words and their definitions located in Appendix B. After you are comfortable with the definitions, complete the exercises. (If you are already familiar with the meaning of each word, you can skip these exercises.)

> **Directions: Read the words in the left column and then find the corresponding definition for each in the right column. Write the letter of the correct definition next to the word. (Answers for each exercise group are listed at the end of the exercises.) After you have finished each exercise, compare your answers to the correct answers at the end of this section. If you missed matching any words to their definitions, simply review that information until you know you have it memorized.**

EXERCISE 1

1. Hassled	a) feeling that someone is out to get you
2. Pressured	b) careful to watch for warning signs
3. Controlled	c) high alert, self-preservation
4. Threatened	d) someone won't leave you alone
5. Trapped	e) feeling the need to protect
6. Uncertain	f) you feel like a puppet
7. Cautious	g) no way out
8. Suspicious	h) requires immediate attention
9. Defensive	i) not feeling sure about things
10. Guarded	j) problems trusting others

EXERCISE 2

1. Embarrassed	a) not organized
2. Foolish	b) beating yourself up, feeling no good
3. Stupid	c) feeling there is no way out
4. Degraded	d) unable to make sense
5. Humiliated	e) downgrade a person in public
6. Scattered	f) have no idea of what is going on
7. Disorganized	g) make someone uneasy in front of others
8. Puzzled	h) put yourself down, not capable of rational thought
9. Confused	i) problems with focusing on one's thoughts
10. Lost	j) feeling uncomfortable, like you did the wrong thing

EXERCISE 3

1. Lonely	a) others run out and do not come back
2. Left Out	b) feeling hurt because you are not included
3. Rejected	c) your expectation does not happen
4. Deserted	d) overwhelmed because you do not matter
5. Abandoned	e) do not give any attention on purpose
6. Disappointed	f) lack of contact with others
7. Frustrated	g) tell a person no: totally ignore
8. Ignored	h) left all by yourself, causing an empty feeling
9. Unimportant	i) hinders you from getting what you want
10. Crushed	j) overlooked because you don't matter

EXERCISE 4

1. Sad	a) disregards one's feelings
2. Empty	b) to be a traitor, trust is impossible
3. Depressed	c) not feeling good
4. Dejected	d) pain from a person or event
5. Defeated	e) trick someone to take advantage of
6. Offended	f) feeling hollow inside
7. Deceived	g) fail to succeed, feel like a failure
8. Used	h) so low that you feel unmotivated
9. Hurt	i) someone gets what they want at your expense
10. Betrayed	j) take it personally, hard to go on

EXERCISE 5

1. Tense	a) beyond control, overwhelmed
2. Nervous	b) lacks confidence in oneself
3. Anxious	c) hope is nowhere to be found
4. Frantic	d) feeling uptight, not relaxed
5. Hysterical	e) can't stand up for oneself
6. Insecure	f) get all worked up, trouble controlling oneself
7. Lost	h) agitation takes over inside you
8. Helpless	g) in a state of desperation
9. Hopeless	i) totally on the wrong track
10. Despair	j) hopelessness at its lowest

EXERCISE 6

1. Apprehensive	a) the show of pleasure
2. Scared	b) stun with fear, you can't move
3. Frightened	c) upset about what could happen
4. Terrified	d) great joy, on cloud nine
5. Petrified	e) strike fear into
6. Good	f) spirits are at their highest
7. Happy	g) you feel terror
8. Excited	h) being satisfied, feeling pleasant
9. Overjoyed	i) a sudden intense feeling of fear
10. Elated	j) feel very enthusiastic

EXERCISE 7

1. Kind	a) showing love or great care, devoted
2. Considerate	b) purposeful, having one's mind made up
3. Caring	c) friendly, generous
4. Affectionate	d) give your attention, caught up in
5. Loving	e) thoughtful, unselfish
6. Willing	f) having great enjoyment, passionate
7. Involved	g) concern for others
8. Determined	h) agreeable, do it because it is your choice
9. Energetic	i) devoted, tender
10. Enthusiastic	j) involving great energy, dynamic

EXERCISE 8

1. Good	a) things are going alright for the moment
2. Wanted	b) worth a great deal, highly prized
3. Important	c) satisfied
4. Honored	d) people want you around
5. Valuable	e) being sure of oneself
6. Okay	f) great respect
7. Content	g) free from fear, care doubt and anxiety
8. Confident	h) having great significance, mean a great deal
9. Safe	i) free from uncomfortable events
10. Secure	j) protected from danger or risk

ANSWERS

EXERCISE 1	EXERCISE 2	EXERCISE 3
1. Hassled—d	1. Embarrassed—g	1. Lonely—f
2. Pressured—h	2. foolish—j	2. left out—b
3. Controlled—f	3. Stupid—h	3. Rejected—g
4. Threatened—a	4. Degraded—b	4. Deserted—h
5. Trapped—g	5. Humiliated—e	5. Abandoned—e
6. Uncertain—i	6. Scattered—i	6. Disappointed—c
7. Cautious—b	7. Disorganized—a	7. Frustrated—i
8. Suspicious—j	8. Puzzled—d	8. Ignored—e
9. Defensive—e	9. Confused—f	9. Unimportant—j
10. Guarded—c	10. Lost—c	10. Crushed—d

EXERCISE 4	EXERCISE 5	EXERCISE 6
1. Sad—c	1. Tense—d	1. Apprehensive—c
2. Empty—f	2. Nervous—f	2. Scared—e
3. Depressed—h	3. Anxious—h	3. Frightened—i
4. Dejected—j	4. Frantic—g	4. Terrified—g
5. Defeated—g	5. Hysterical—a	5. Petrified—b
6. Offended—a	6. Insecure—b	6. Good—h
7. Deceived—e	7. Helpless—e	7. Happy—a
8. Used—l	8. Lost—l	8. Excited—j
9. Hurt—d	9. Hopeless—c	9. Overjoyed—d
10. Betrayed—b	10. Despair—j	10. Elated—f

EXERCISE 7	EXERCISE 8
1. Kind—c	1. Good—i
2. Considerat—e	2. Wanted—d
3. Caring— g	3. Important—h
4. Affectionate—I	4. Honored—f
5. Loving—a	5. Valuable—b
6. Willing— h	6. Okay—a
7. Involved—d	7. Content—c
8. Determined—b	8. Confident—e
9. Energetic— j	9. Safe—j
10. Enthusiastic—f	10. Secure—g

Anchors and Mountains—How to Use Them

ANGER IS A SIGNIFICANT PART OF OUR LIVES. As we learned earlier, anger is also part of the grieving process. When you face a loss, waves of feelings referred to as *grief*, attack your innermost being. You may feel isolated, alone, depressed or like you're falling apart and having a nervous breakdown. Your feelings overwhelm you. As explained previously, this is when it is so easy to block your feelings, to suppress them, and that can be harmful. Just be aware that sometimes it is okay to delay feeling, but you will, in time, need to feel and cope with them. You can use the anchors (explained later) on the following pages to get in touch with your feelings, then you can channel them into more productive endeavors. This bears repeating: *Painful feelings that are left inside us, without attention, become stronger, cause distortions in our perceptions of the world, and evolve into physical attacks on our body, including depression. Acknowledgment of our feelings is critical. Denying that our feelings exist is self-defeating.*

Awareness of feelings for every encounter that requires a reaction is the first step in the art of problem-solving. Once a feeling is identified, only then are you able to determine your course of action. When you become skilled in that identification, you will make better decisions for both yourself and others, and you will find the appropriate course of action for situations.

The anchors are used in this book to help you identify the intensity of your feelings. In our visualization exercise, we will descend to the ocean floor as we explore a range of emotions. There are sixteen categories with five feelings listed on each one, and ranked from less severe to the most severe. There are many feelings that are not listed in this exercise, but you should be able to learn how to identify them by using this same procedure. Two emotions that were left out on purpose are shame and guilt, but both have their place in the world of feelings. They would be at the bottom, buried in the ocean floor. This is why they were omitted.

Let's take the time to go over a few of the anchors before you continue. The first illustration is labeled "When I'm backed into a corner, I feel…" The feelings that are attached to the corresponding anchor range from 1 to 5, with one being the least intense and five being the most intense. They include: 1) hassled 2) pressured 3) controlled 4) threatened 5) trapped. The deeper you travel down the anchor, the more intense the feeling. The anchor helps you to identify and analyze your feelings and their source, which is on the opposite page. Problematic as this might be, most people are generally unaware of what they are feeling and why. Learning the skills presented in this chapter can improve personal awareness, communication skills, and interpersonal relationships.

Next, look at the feelings attached to the anchor associated with the category "When people are out to get me, I feel…" They are 1) uncertain 2) cautious 3) suspicious 4) defensive 5) guarded. Once again, the deeper you do down (the higher the number), the more intense the feeling.

There are eleven categories for unpleasant and five categories for pleasant feelings. As you complete this next exercise, think back to anger rule nine: "anger protects us from painful feelings." As we learned earlier, this is the reason why we get angry—to protect ourselves temporarily until we are able to cope. See how they are listed on the corresponding anchors

Anchors and Scenarios

Applying General Situations

Go through each category and illustration. Do this several times so you can get an overall understanding of the various categories and the associated feelings. Remember, the anchors are made up of painful feelings. The further you go down, the greater the intensity. The positive feelings are listed on mountains. The higher you ascend, the more intense the feeling. Again, in these illustrations, a number one means the least intense. The number 5 means the most intense.

At the end of the categories, the feelings and illustrations relate more to everyday situations. As you read them, look back at the anchors and mountains. Try to find the category that fits the situation. Then find the words that best describe the feelings in each category. What is the intensity of the feeling? The lower you go on the anchor, the more complicated the problem solving and putting it into action. Once you complete all of the scenarios, start using this exercise for situations you find yourself in every day.

When I'm backed into a corner I feel ...

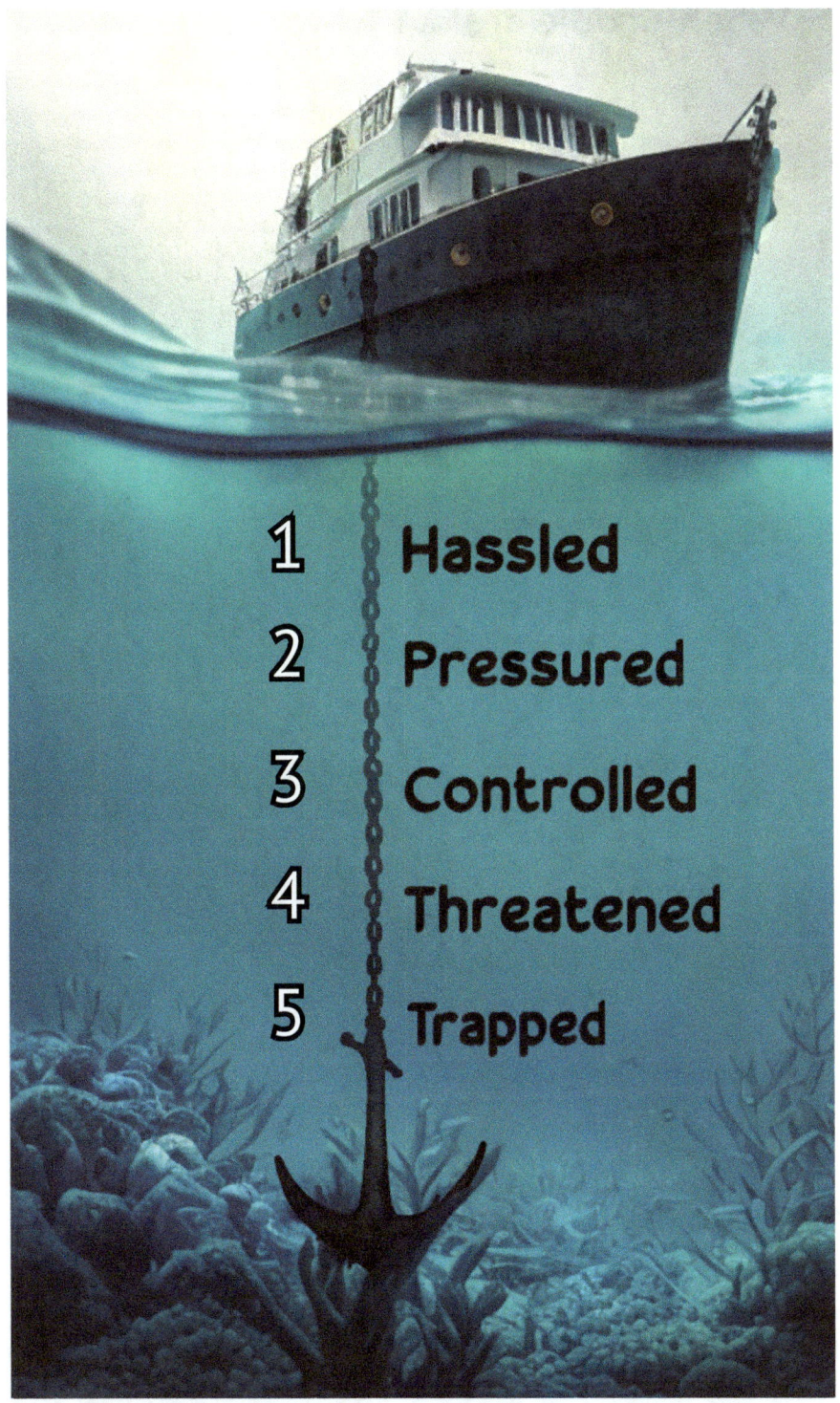

When people are out to get me I feel...

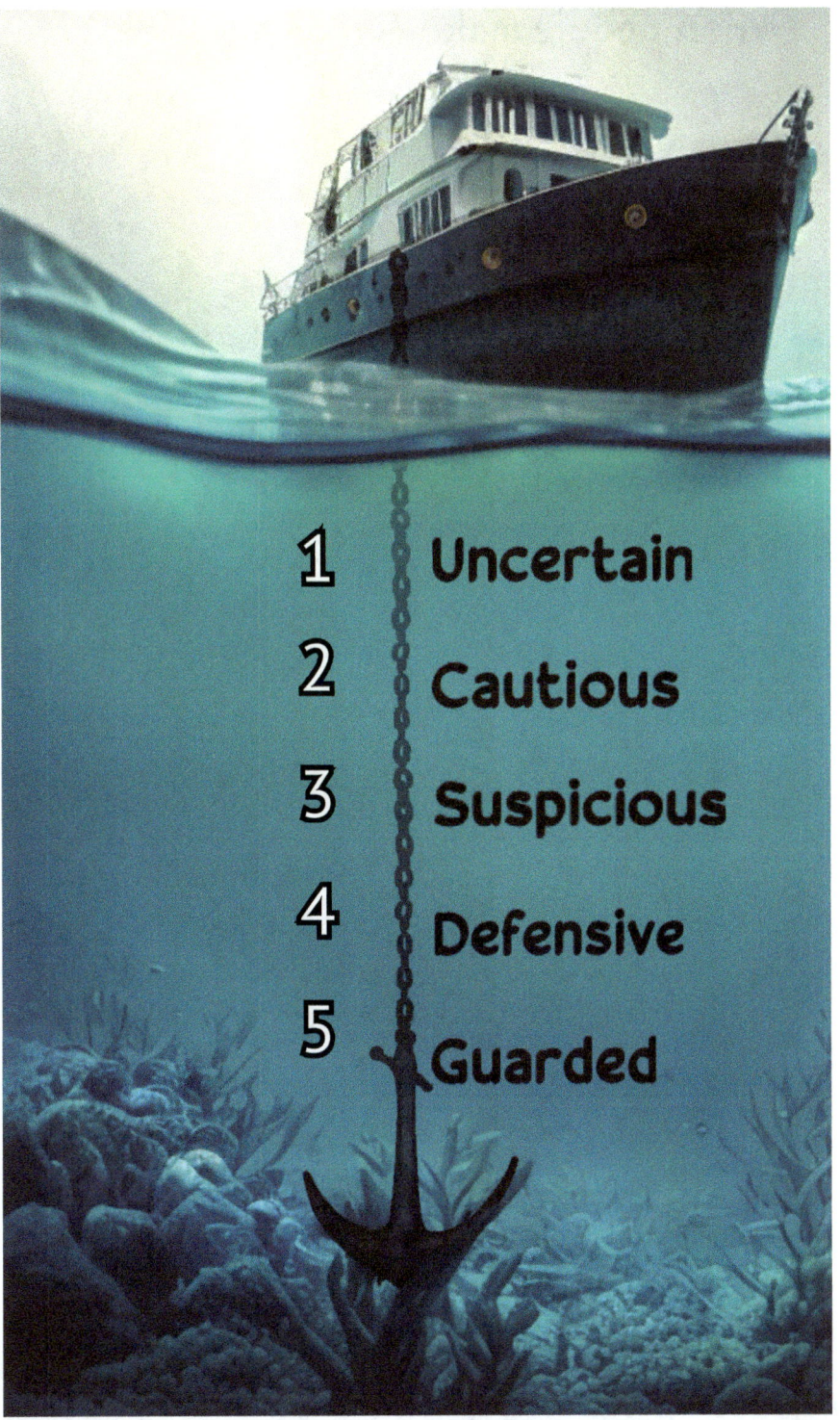

When people make fun of me I feel...

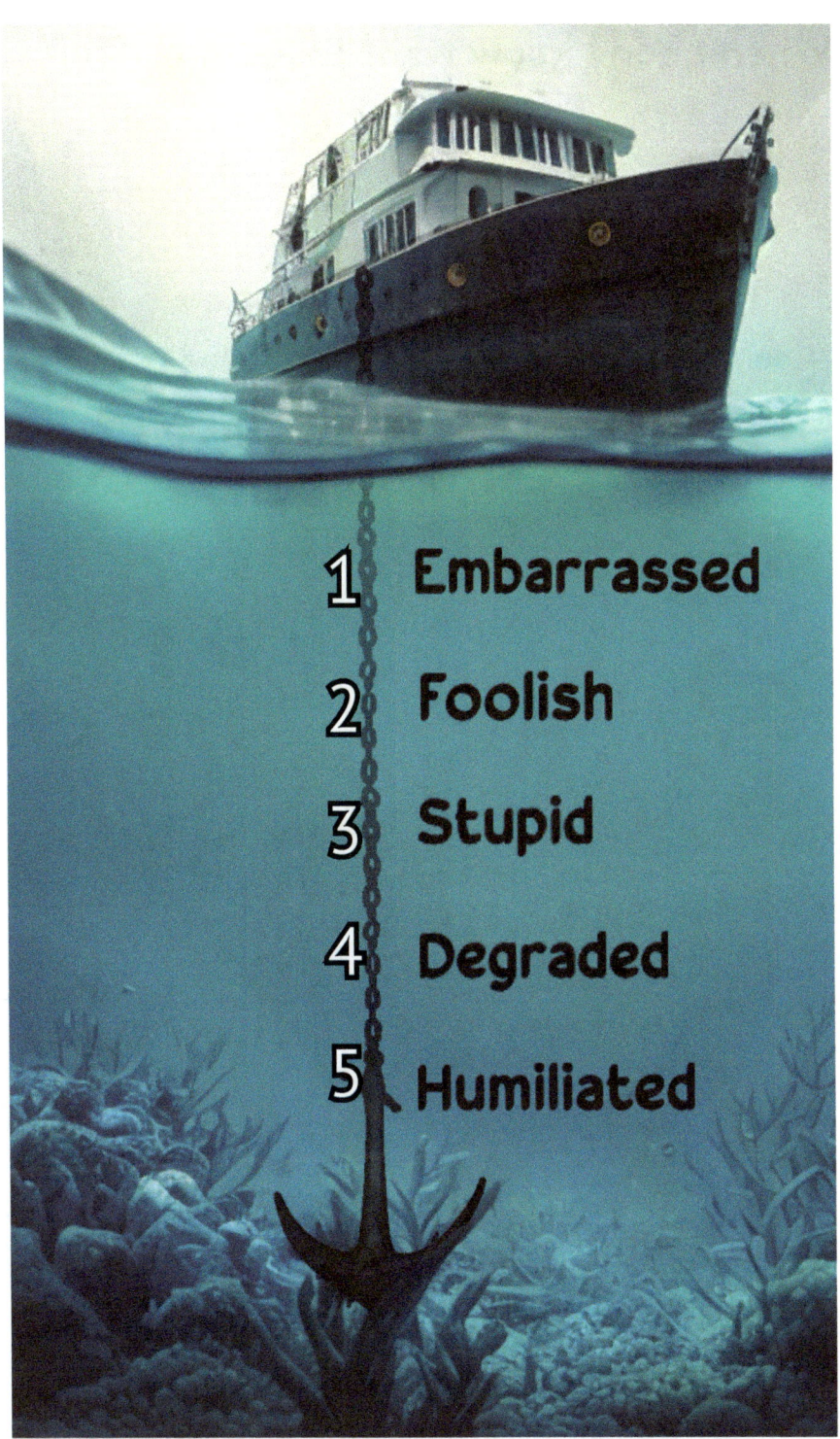

When I don't know what I'm doing I feel...

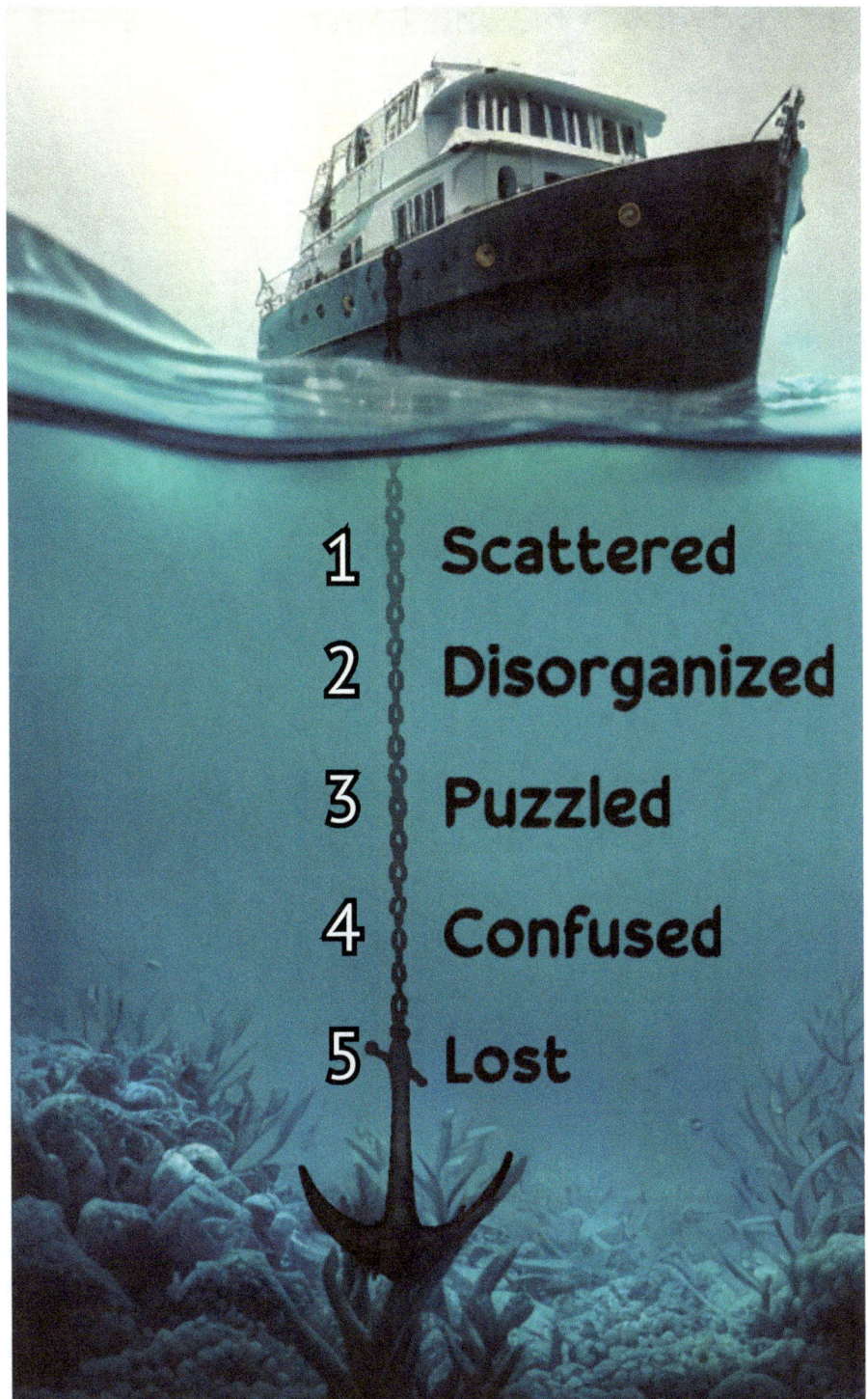

Nobody loves me and I feel...

When you let me down I feel...

When nothing goes my way I feel...

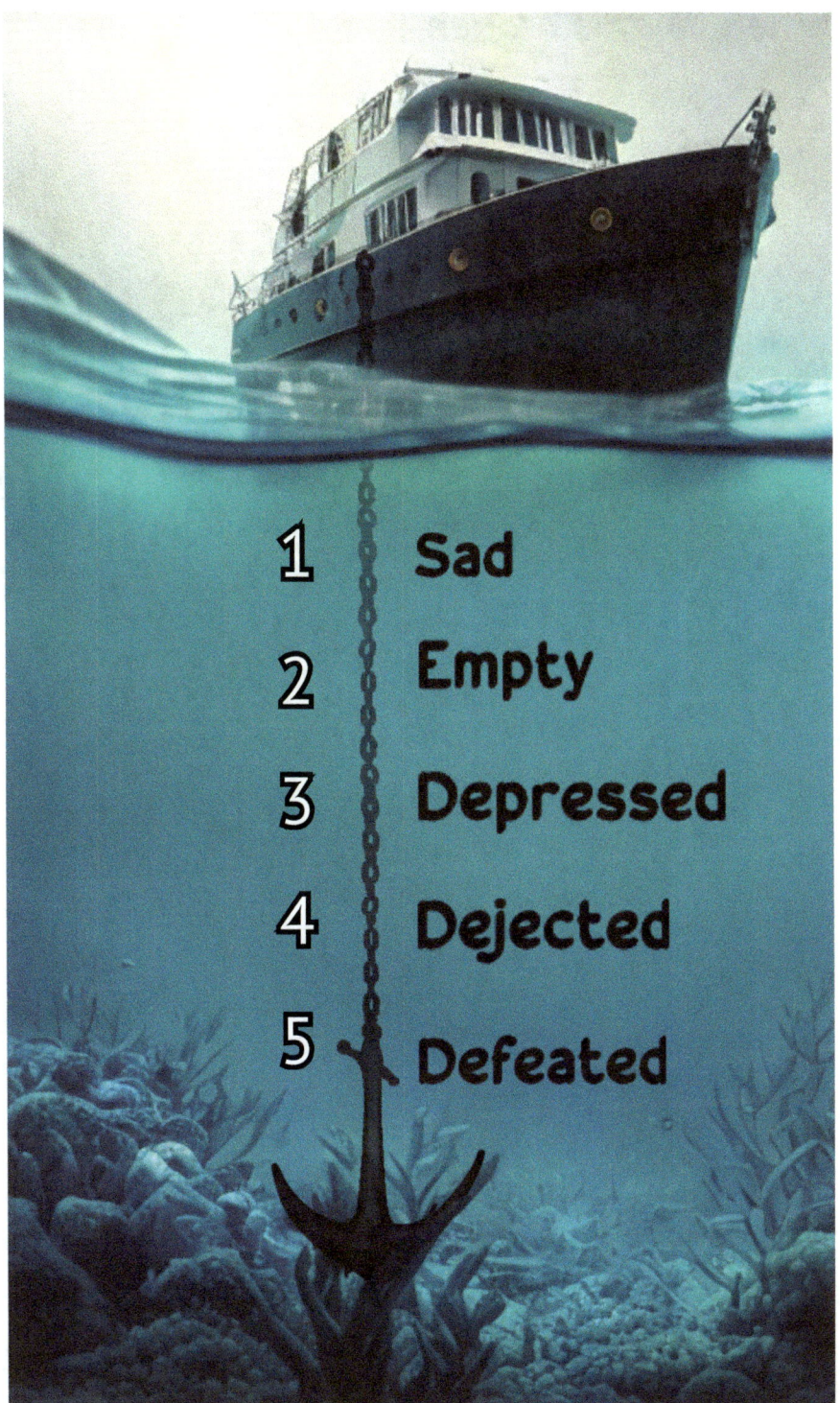

When trust is broken I feel...

When I just can't win I feel...

When worry is inside me I feel . . .

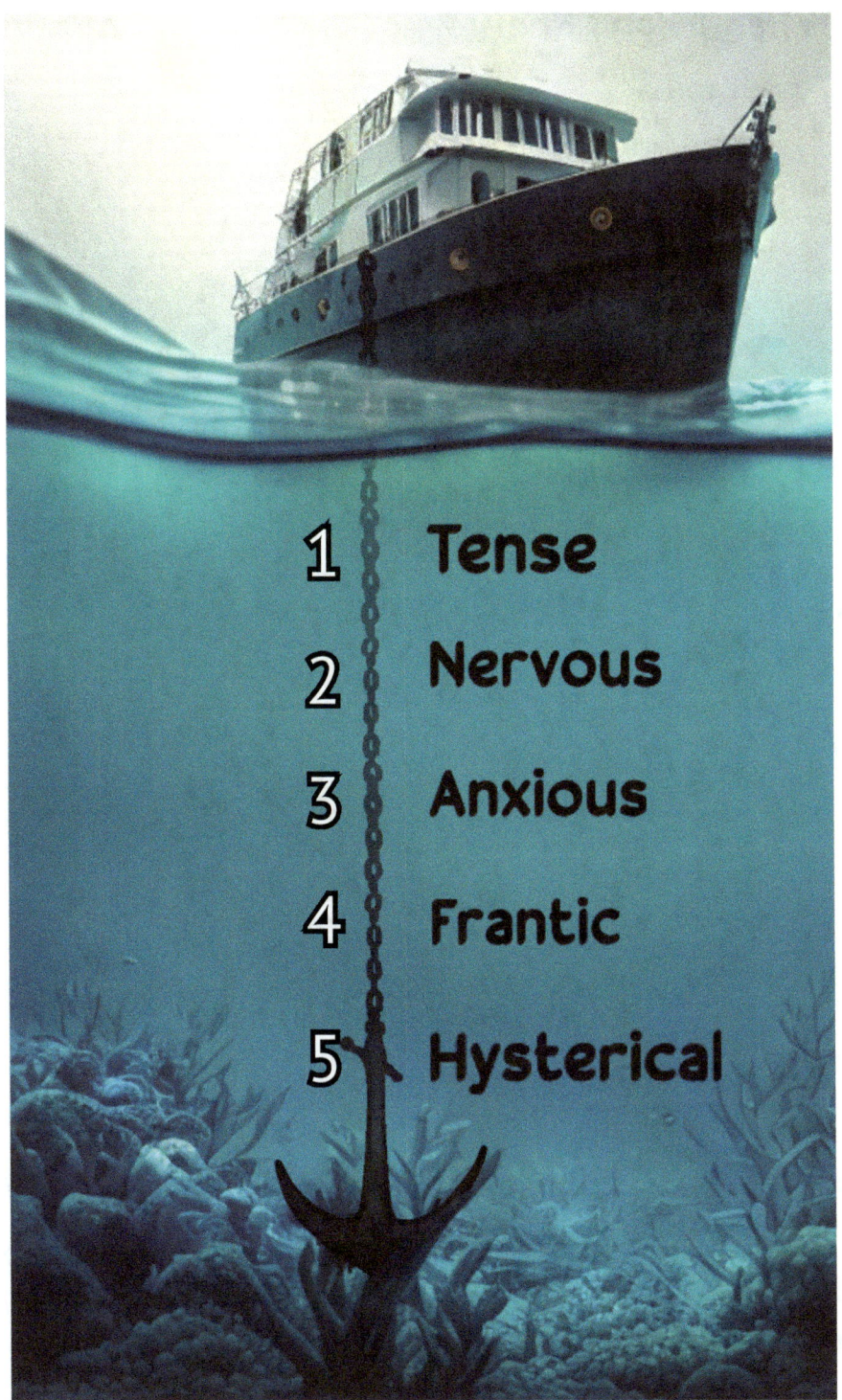

When I don't know what is about to happen I feel...

When things are going my way I feel...

When I show respect to others I feel...

When I do things I like I feel...

When I'm praised I feel...

When it is all right to give my opinion I feel...

Examples

- **It's noon time and the students are in the cafeteria.** Alfonsa sits down with some of her classmates. Billy, the joker in school, joins them at the table. Alfonsa wore a new dress that she bought last weekend and it did look somewhat questionable in taste. Billy immediately starts to ridicule her. He goes on and on about the dress and how she looks in it. At this point, Alfonsa is embarrassed. This falls under the category of "When people make fun of me." On a five-point scale, it is only one. Action can be implemented quickly. She could be assertive and tell him to stop or she could move to another table. The important thing is to identify the feeling and determine an appropriate course of action. She moves to another table.

- **Tommy is taking an introductory chemistry class.** Overwhelmed, he still attends class every day and puts forth his best effort to understand the information. Morning rolls around, the alarm goes off and Tommy dreads getting out of bed, all the while he is thinking about chemistry. He eventually begins skipping class. He wallows in a state of denial. After a considerable degree of suffering and guilt, Tommy admits that "When I don't know what I'm doing, I feel…" Lost is the best word to describe the dilemma. Looking at the anchor, he notices that the feeling of lost is a 5, the most intense. Tommy decides on a course of action. He could get help from a classmate, get help from the professor or drop the class. Which one would be best for him? Only Tommy knows the answer. He drops the class since his stress is too high.

- **Roger is in his third month at a youth center for delinquent adolescents.** The staff is trying to teach him to problem-solve, but he still doesn't understand and has little insight. He is constantly being reprimanded. The counselor had been meeting with him over the last couple of weeks. Together, they identified his problem category as, "When I just can't win, I feel…" He chose the feeling of hopelessness from the chart, which is number 4. The staff used this recognition of feeling hopeless to help him with his problem-solving strategy and to build it into his treatment plan. (When I was working at the youth center in Osawatomie, oftentimes I found those who graduated from the program after being able to identify feelings, used positive self-talk to assess their options and problem-solve.)

- **Born in Nicaragua, Maria is attending her first dance in middle school.** Being a refugee in her first year at an American school, she has only made one other friend, a girl of her own ethnicity. Upon entering the auditorium, Maria is uneasy with the loud music, the commotion, and the crowd of students. Luckily, she receives moral support from her friend. An hour passes while students mingle, dance, and laugh with the friends in their cliques. Maria enjoys the music, but the atmosphere starts to become overwhelming. She is concerned about what people think of her. She selected the category of "When worry is inside me, I feel…" to express what she was feeling. Anxious was the feeling that she identified, which was a level three. Even though she was anxious, she was able to cope with the situation by being with her friend and taking a few breaks outside. The solution was to take short time-outs and leave a little early.

- **Tanya's parents are very strict.** She is not to be out later than 8 pm on weeknights and 11 pm on weekends. She finally lands a date with the guy she has had a crush on for months. He picks her up around seven. He meets her parents and they leave on a positive note. After they eat dinner, go to a movie, and spend some time with his friends, it is around 1 am when she gets home. As she enters the house, she encounters two hostile parents awaiting her arrival. Her mind immediately went to "When I'm backed into a corner, I feel..." and she thought of a strong level 5—trapped. What was the solution? She needed help. The next day she went to the counselor's office at school. She was able to release some of her feelings and tried to control her anger toward her parents. When she regained control of her anger, the counselor requested a meeting with her and her parents. The parents were still resistive, but they extended her curfew to midnight.

- **Shelly was having difficulty at school.** That was to put it mildly. She was a transfer student and this was her sophomore year. She had a history of having problems with all of the schools she attended. Her parents moved around a lot, and she could never get settled down in any of the places. Finally, her parents took her to a mental health center. After therapy, it was revealed she was drowning in shame and guilt. Neither of these is on our charts, but they are mentioned in this book. It takes a trained mental health worker to identify these emotions and determine a course of action. After a month of therapy, it was discovered that she had been sexually abused over a six-month period at the age of eight. She had endured this in silence until now.

- **Daniel is a seventh grader in middle school. He was diagnosed with a learning disability in second grade.** Four of his teachers had given him homework to be completed the next day. He completed them but left one at home and one in his locker. The important thing is that he completed them. This came under the category, "When I don't know what I'm doing, I feel..." It was a level two—not organized. He came up with a plan. For the class that he left the assignment at home, he went to the teacher and explained his dilemma. For the one in the locker, he asked to be permitted to go get it.

Hopefully, you now understand the procedure and it's time to practice. In the next series of scenarios, try to identify the categories and corresponding feelings. Relax. There are no right or wrong answers. Only you can recognize the feelings inside of you. This is the beginning of the identification process and a prelude to problem-solving.

- **Anita has completed her senior year of high school.** Her parents are driving her to a college they have selected for her. Upon pulling up to the dorm, she encounters a diverse group of students. She is from a small town where everyone was pretty much the same and everyone knew what everyone was doing. She is ready to enter the dorm. What category does she fall under? What feeling is inside of her?

- **Ethan has spent the day at his job, putting in about 10 hours. He is tired but needs some time for his personal enjoyment.** He calls his friends and they meet in the park. They hang out and talk to each other while listening to music. Before long, a police car pulls up. Two policemen get out and start asking them questions. They feel like they are being interrogated. Ethan wonders if the reason could be that they are African-American. What category does this fall under? What feeling is inside of him?

- **Keenan is currently going to school and doing a part-time job at the same time.** He is saving to buy his own car. His grades have been slipping and his parents are concerned about his school performance. They believe his job is the cause and they tell him he has to quit. He is adamant that isn't the reason. His opinion is the opposite of his parents. He needs that job. What category does this fall under? What feeling is inside of him?

Applying the Situation to Your Life

Exercise Set #1

- *Your mother has been diagnosed with cancer.* **The doctor informed the family that she is in an advanced stage. What category does this fall under? What feeling is inside of you?**

- *A friend of yours agrees to go to an upcoming concert.* **The day comes to buy tickets and she says she has made other plans. What category does this fall under? What feeling is inside of you?**

- *After the school play was over, the drama club went out to celebrate.* **You were part of the cast, but you were not invited. What category does this fall under? What feeling is inside of you?**

- *You are participating in the gymnastics competition.* **You are about to perform your floor exercise. This is a difficult routine for you. The team scores are close. Your performance may make the difference in the competition. What category does this fall under? What feeling is inside of you?**

- *You took first place in the cross-country meet.* **At the school assembly, you are called to come up to the stage before the entire school body and be presented with your medal. What category does this fall under? What feeling is inside you?**

- *You are unjustly accused of shoplifting.* **The store owner takes you to the back room in the store and starts to interrogate you. What category does this fall under? What feeling is inside of you?**

- *At the swim meet, you come in second place.* **What category does this fall under? What is the feeling inside of you?**
- *You are home alone and you hear someone trying to get into the house.* **What category does this fall under? What is the feeling inside of you?**
- *You are the victim of cyberbullying.* **You get a derogatory message every night. What category does this fall under? What is the feeling inside of you?**
- *An assignment in geometry was given to the class.* **That evening you try your best, but you miss many of the answers. What category does this fall under? What is the feeling inside of you?**
- *It's February 25th, your birthday.* **None of your friends remember it. What category does this fall under? What is the feeling inside of you?**

Exercise Set #2

- *It's already one in the morning.* **You lost track of the time and you sneak in the back door. Your father is waiting for you. He begins to raise his voice and tell you how irresponsible you are. What category does this fall under? What is the feeling inside of you?**
- *The alarm clock rings.* **You are half asleep and you turn it off. Thirty minutes later, you wake up and realize you're late for school. You get in your car and the gas tank is empty so you have to stop by the gas station. You finally get to school and you have trouble opening your locker. You make it to your second-hour class, but you are late for it. You now have to go to the office and get a permission slip. What category does this fall under? What is the feeling inside of you?**

- *You are on the baseball team.* **A fly ball comes your way and you drop it. What category does this fall under? What is the feeling inside of you?**

- *Problems at home.* **You have to tell someone, so you confide in your best friend. The next day, you discover that she told it to someone else. What category does this fall under? What is the feeling inside of you?**

- *Your grandfather died.* **You were very close to him. What category does this fall under? What is the feeling inside of you?**

- *The teacher told you that you were one of his best students in his class.* **What category does this fall under? What is the feeling inside of you?**

- *Everyone seems to pick on me.* **I can't help it if I look kind of goofy. It's nothing I can change. What category does this fall under? What is the feeling inside of you?**

- *It is the eve of your first judo match.* **You have been practicing for weeks, but you are going up against a skilled opponent. What category does this fall under? What is the feeling inside of you?**

- *There are some gangs near your neighborhood.* **They have watched you on several occasions when you were walking down the street. What category does this fall under? What feeling is inside of you?**

- *You try and you try and you try, and you still can't get it.* **What category does this fall under? What is the feeling inside of you?**

- *You get to go to the lake this weekend and go water skiing for the first time.* **What category does this fall under? What is the feeling inside of you?**

Exercise Set #3

- *Wow! This has been a great day!* **What category does this fall under? What is the feeling inside of you?**
- *You're on a camping trip and a tarantula falls from a tree onto your face.* **What category does this fall under? What is the feeling inside you?**
- *You broke your curfew while on probation and are standing before the judge.* **What category does this fall under? What is the feeling inside of you?**
- *You are going to do platform diving for the first time.* **What category does this fall under? What is the feeling inside of you?**
- *Your GPS leads you to the wrong destination.* **What category does this fall under? What is the feeling inside of you?**
- *You tested positive for COVID.* **What category does this fall under? What is the feeling inside of you?**
- *You interviewed for a part-time job and were hired.* **What category does this fall under? What is the feeling inside of you?**
- *You were finally able to purchase your first car.* **What category does this fall under? What is the feeling inside of you?**
- *You have received special education services since first grade.* **Now you are a freshman. You still struggle. What category does this fall under? What is the feeling inside of you?**
- *You have a drinking problem.* **You are a borderline alcoholic. What category do you fall under? What is the feeling inside of you?**
- **They are taking X-rays to determine the severity of the damage. What category does this fall under? What is the feeling inside of you?**

Chapter 5: It's All About Character!

What Are Your Character Traits?

What kind of person do you want to be? That is the decision that you have to make for yourself. There are many encounters that you will come up against throughout your life. They will be full of challenges. How you handle them will determine the person that you will become.

We have already explored feelings and how they affect you. With that knowledge, you are able to use self-analysis and decision making in regard to the problems you face. You have the tools to make informed decisions that could possibly help yourself and others. Spend time each day going through what you have learned and you will be ready for the next step—the acquisition of virtues.

Virtues are qualities that are sought after by even the wisest of men. Justice, tolerance, patience, kindness, reliability, truthfulness, and trustworthiness are but a few. You seek to acquire these attributes to enhance your character and contribute to the greater good of others. By practicing these noble virtues, you define who you are and what you stand for, thus improving the possibility of reaching your full potential. Character building requires effort and continued practice. A relationship terminated due to the death of someone close, or losing something meaningful to you can cause pain and sorrow, but they are also occasions to lay a groundwork for self-improvement. How you handle difficult times and stress ironically provides you with opportunities to build upon your character development.

How We Assess Virtues

THE UNITED STATES OF AMERICA IS UNDOUBTEDLY the greatest country in the world—at least this sentiment is felt by most Americans. Comprised of immigrants from all nationalities and religions, our diversity defines our greatness. Sure, the United States has its flaws and imperfections, but it strives to protect equal rights and the pursuit of happiness for all of its citizens. Our country proudly proclaims freedom for all. We are a nation of values and ideals. Just read the Preamble of the Constitution which advocates justice and equality, and sets the tone for how our great sovereignty operates.

> *We the People of the United States, in Order to form a more perfect Union, establish Justice, insure domestic Tranquility, provide for the common defense, promote the general Welfare, and secure the Blessings of Liberty to ourselves and our Posterity, do ordain and establish this Constitution for the United States of America.*

The very foundation, the inner core of this country, is founded on our values, virtues, and principles.

The next step in our transformation program is to look within ourselves. Be honest. Take the assessment on page 195 to determine your strengths and weaknesses. Are you satisfied with your results? Where can you make improvements?

Discover areas that you wish to improve. Keep a simple record of the virtues that you are to work on for each particular day. Pick three so as not to become overwhelmed. Set goals for yourself

and become disciplined. To be successful keep the record-keeping and goals simple and easy to practice.

Visualization Exercise

Picture in your mind a magnificent gallery full of art of unspeakable beauty. Pictures and statues are beyond comprehension and imagination. Upon entering the front corridor, you discover a bright and radiant room that is filled with light, music, and large picture windows that overlook a garden of flowers, trees, fountains, and wildlife. Works of art, representative of the virtues that we are studying, are spread throughout the gallery. Imagine each piece of art is a virtue that represents a challenge for us to incorporate into our lives. Begin the tour in the center of the room where you discover one of the primary objects—the statue of justice.

Justice

Justice is a virtue of high importance, defined as the act of being morally right and fair. Its power shines as an example of unity and peace among the people and countries of the world. Without justice, you have anarchy and unrest. Practicing this virtue entails being fair in all situations, judging events in a non-bipartisan manner, and making sure all people have equal rights. Justice is necessary if we are to achieve peacefulness and orderliness. There are two basic principles involved with this virtue—reward and punishment. With justice, you can correct iniquities, falsehoods, and harmful practices to make this world a better place for all. This virtue delivers the message to each of us to be careful of our words and actions, not to harm another living soul.

Visualization Exercise

Continuing on in the gallery, we enter a rather large room that is separate from the others. There you find the special virtues of faith, hope, and love. Their radiance overpowers the other virtues and provides you with a purpose in life. Devoid and empty, the world would lose much of its meaning, creating roadblocks to our eternal path, without them.

Faith

When we think of trust, we think of faith. This virtue has the potency to open our eyes and make things happen beyond our wildest dreams. The impossible becomes possible. Most often, faith is associated with a belief in a higher power.

Prayer is one example of faith put in action, where we give praise, seek forgiveness, and on occasion make special requests. Faith is the foundation for believing in an incomprehensible Creator, whose responses to our prayers are not always recognizable, but are heard and will result in action to benefit us. Many people believe that our faith in the power of prayer, is real and beneficial. You might recognize the little prayer from when you were growing up, "Now I Lay Me Down to Sleep" by John Adams.

"Now I lay me down to sleep,

I pray the Lord my soul to keep,

If I should die before I wake,

I pray the Lord my soul to take."

This prayer illustrates faith in action. A further example of faith is the story about Albert Ellis.

Story

Albert Ellis, a famous psychologist who created rational emotive therapy, had to learn to have faith in himself. While growing up, he had parents who neglected him, not giving him the love that he needed. He often had to care for his two younger siblings. Health was also a real issue for him. Between the ages of 5 and 7, he was hospitalized eight times, and one of these lasted 10 months. Do you think his parents took the time to visit? Rarely!

In his younger days, he considered himself shy. In his late teenage years, he decided to develop faith in himself. At first, he had difficulty in his interactions with women so he decided to do something about it. In one-month, he spoke to over 100 women in the park, but experienced many rejections. In fact, only one agreed to go out with him and she didn't even show up for the date. Despite these failures, he continued to push forward in faith.

Surprisingly, after all of these encounters with women, Albert became confident in himself. He was no longer shy. He believed in himself. He learned to speak before large audiences. And he eventually got married. After taking courses in business and writing in college, he trained in the area of psychoanalysis. He became disinterested in it because of its passive approach to people's problems He believed that the therapist needed to take a more focused, active part in the process and consequently developed his own form of treatment as noted earlier-rational emotive therapy. it was more focused, with the patient taking an active role. This led him to become one of the most famous psychoanalysts.

Faith does make a difference. Even with a challenging background full of hardships and painful encounters. Developing faith in yourself can help you achieve your goals and find happiness in your life.

Faith is not limited to belief in a Higher Power. We can have faith in ourselves and in others. Perhaps having faith in ourselves is the most difficult to achieve. It is shaped by our parents and by the important people in our lives. The love and positive feedback we received from them strengthened us. We learn to have confidence in ourselves as we seek to help others. We also have faith in others by getting to know them and establishing bonds of trust and dependability. It is the power of positive thinking put into its highest form. As discovered when reviewing self-talk, faith is contained in the words we think and speak because we *are* what we think and speak.

Faith is used in other ways too. Remember the movie ***Indiana Jones and the Last Crusade?*** It was released in 1989. In case you have never seen the movie, Indiana Jones played by Harrison Ford, in his quest to get the Holy Grail, came upon a deep, gigantic ravine that separated him from the chamber that held the chalice. According to the ancient writings, Indy had to take a leap of faith in order to traverse the crevice. Just upon observation with the human eye, it would appear that Indy would certainly fall to his death if he took a step off the cliff. After taking a deep breath and meditating on the writings, he stepped forward and a previously invisible ramp and walkway appeared, allowing him to find the chalice. No matter how hopeless it might seem in overcoming our fears, bad habits, and painful feelings, there is a pathway called faith that can lead us to happiness and self-improvement. What you believe is where you put your faith.

In the Rocky movies, in order to win, Rocky needed to train hard, but more importantly, believe in himself. He needed faith—the eye of the tiger. In **Rocky III** (1982), when things were getting rough, you could hear Rocky's corner man yell at him, "He's just a man!" He also yelled, "Eye of the tiger," reminding Rocky to have faith in himself and give it his best.

Isn't there a time in your life that you have found faith? Do you have faith in your best friend? In your church? In God? In your parents? Do you have faith in yourself? Restore or build upon your faith in yourself and take action. When you take that step, you begin the journey to strengthen your character, develop your virtues, become productive, and capable of helping yourself and others. Next you can start the process of focusing on the positive which will naturally reduce the negative. Complete trust, confidence, belief, or conviction in someone or something is what we need to go forward in faith and make things happen.

Hope

HOPE—AS A PEOPLE, WE MUST HAVE it. Hope is one of those virtues that is crucial for our survival. Without hope, depression and darkness overcome the body and mind. Just imagine if we eliminated all of the hope in the world. The world would stay as it is or get worse. There would be no hope of ending all the wars that are going on. There would be no hope of us growing and becoming better people. What if there was no hope in your life? No matter who you ask on date, the answer is always no. You play cards with your friends and always have the same losing hand. No matter what you do, your situation will not improve or it could get worse. Without hope, you might as well quit because you are already defeated.

There are those children who learn early in their homes or in school that they have little hope, just more disappointments. At home, they see their parents fight and argue day after day. Perhaps they live in a home with an alcoholic parent. Then there is divorce, another struggle for them. What if they are orphans and are deprived of having any parents? Worse yet, they may be the victims of abuse and neglect. In school, they may have to cope with the other children who tell them that they are stupid, that they are ugly, or fat. Their peers may make fun of their race, religion, or ethnicity. These bullying comments attack self-esteem, stifling hope. This attack can come from the home, school, or neighborhood. In middle school attacks may become even worse as children become teenagers. Cyberbullying begins to complicate the issue. There is an environment where being different can result in additional attacks on one's self-esteem, even isolation. By the end of high school, there are those students who leave with a shaky self-concept, their hope underdeveloped, and their potential hidden within. Hope must be kept alive and thriving in all children, adolescents, and adults.

Hope was embodied within the Hindu man named Gandhi in 1930s India. His countrymen found themselves under British rule, enduring anti-Indian laws and unfair practices. Yearning for freedom, they were a people with little or no hope. Then, this small Indian man, not more than 110 pounds in weight, caught the imagination of a country. He became a spokesperson and a leader for independence, instilling hope into millions as he advocated for freedom. Gandhi was described as a good man who fought for the independence of India from British rule. The Indian people referred to him as Mahatma, meaning great soul. He advocated a non-violent approach to gaining independence while making sure that British soldiers were not harmed in the process. When one of his campaigns turned violent, Gandhi demanded that it be called off and he went into fasting. He endured many hardships, including a total of 12 years in prison, but his peacekeeping efforts were finally rewarded. One of his gifts to the Indian people was hope and India gained independence from Britain on August 15, 1947.

Hope is a necessary virtue if we are to achieve and maintain our success and well-being. If hope fades from our grasp, hopelessness settles in. There isn't a more undesirable feeling than hopelessness—there is no sense in trying, things cannot and will not ever change. Our energy leaves us, and our spirit cries out in pain.

What do you do when your spirit is down and the feeling of hopelessness starts to enter your mind? This is a good time to use the visualizations and affirmations that we talked about earlier in the book. Tell yourself that everything is going to be great! Think positively. Get rid of those negative thoughts. Picture yourself having a good time, doing things you use to enjoy. Set a goal for yourself and work towards it. Connect with your family and friends. Stay active with hobbies and things you like to do. It all comes down to this—you have to do something about it.

Love

LOVE—THE MOST POWERFUL VIRTUE ON THE face of the planet. For many, love is first associated with a gift from our Creator to bring joy and fulfillment to our lives. Simply stated, it brings meaning to living life on earth. When you love someone, you care for them and they fill your heart with joy. Consider this virtue in levels. The greatest of all, of course, is the love between our Creator and us. We honor Him, praise Him, are devoted to Him, and love Him. As a result, everlasting love binds us to this unknowable essence. This is love at its highest level.

The next level is family love. Ideally, it starts with the attraction of a man and woman to each other and results in holy matrimony. It then progresses to the love between a husband and wife that leads to the birth of children. This, in turn, leads to children who become a part of their parents. This brings joy with a love that is beyond words. Their progeny make life meaningful and magical. The love of children for their parents is also magical, enduring, and everlasting. Parents have the blessings of watching their children grow up, sharing in their pain and triumphs, and assisting them in their time of need. When their children get married later in life, they have the additional blessing of grandchildren.

Next, there is the love we have for our relatives and friends. We celebrate their victories and are there to mourn with them over their losses. This love emphasizes caring, compassion, patience, consideration and forgiveness—helping each other when in pain, listening to problems, and being there in times of need to give love and support.

Love then marches on as we care about the people of all nations. Unity is the goal, and dignity and respect for everyone is the ultimate outcome. All are equal with no one above anyone else. In all interactions, we must be attentive to treating people with kindness and not harming a living soul. We need to consider ourselves as world citizens, free from prejudices and differences to make this world a better place.

Finally, love is also a connection we have with our pets. Yes, I am talking about animals! We Americans spend a huge amount of money on our pets every year, approximately $109 billion in 2021 according to the American Pet Products Association which also states that at least 70% of U.S. households have at least one pet. Pets become important members of our families. They give us unconditional love and provide us with security. Pets are there to greet us when we get home from a hard day of responsibilities and when we wake up in the morning.

The love that we have spoken of so far binds the world together. Celebrating life, waking up each morning is a special gift that each one of us possesses. Up to this point, love has been illustrated in living things but there are other kinds of love. There is the love of country—most people are patriotic when it comes to supporting the country in which they live. There is the love of a profession—usually felt by those trained in a particular occupation with a dedication to the work and perhaps even fellow workers. Some occupations, in their very nature, are designed with a mission to love and serve; nursing, assisted living caregiving, religious organization outreach, and public and private educators are examples.

I have to take a minute and tell you a story of love. Some of you might have brothers and sisters in elementary school. At LaCygne Elementary, where I had the privilege of serving as principal, there was a new student who enrolled from a previous placement. He was labeled a special needs student who required extensive modifications to be successful. On his first day at school, we discovered that he had some unusual tendencies. He would wander around the room, sometimes crawling by the other students' desks, barking in the faces of his classmates, and refusing to work or do assignments. Spending time under his desk, while classroom instruction was given, was a favorite behavior for him. He had great difficulty making transition from one activity to another, especially at recess when he refused to come back inside the school building after it ended. When things weren't going his way, he ran out into the school hallways, trying to escape the demands of the classroom. So how is this related to love? The cooperative's special education team came together to consult with The University of Kansas. A series of recommendations were proposed. Some were realistic, others were not. The classroom teacher was instructed to give attention to this student every 5—10 minutes. This, of course, created problems while teaching 20 other students in the classroom. It was also recommended that the student should have an entire table for himself, with files to organize his work. The classroom teacher really tried to implement and follow the recommendations. She was a dedicated teacher who put her heart and soul into her work, and was willing to try anything if it meant helping one of her students. Unfortunately, she was unable to carry out the demands of these unrealistic recommendations by herself.

As an alternative strategy, the student received assistance from a paraprofessional and some additional time in the special education resource room. This helped considerably. The student's main advantage was that he was placed in the classroom of a veteran teacher who loved her students, and who would go beyond the limitations imposed by the school. The critical factor, which is often the case for success, was the relationship between the teacher and the student. The power of love was the key. You can do all the right things by making recommendations, but if you don't touch the heart and the spirit of the child, those amazing changes will be minimal and often short-term.

Love opens us up to a host of other virtues, including compassion, helpfulness, trust, forgiveness, patience, kindness, and sincerity. Without love, our life loses its meaning. Without love, meaningful change in our lives is limited and extremely difficult to achieve. We need love to tap into our spiritual power so we can assist and support others with their struggles, reaching out, especially to those who are less fortunate—the homeless, the poor, the handicapped, and the elderly.

Visualization Exercise

CONTINUING ON OUR TOUR, WE FIND OURSELVES entering the Hall of Honor. The paintings on the wall depict such virtues as trust, truthfulness, reverence, honor, and respect. These are the all-important virtues. Without these, it becomes impossible to build a foundation for our character. If we are ever hopeful of working with others in cooperation, if ever to form close friendships, if ever to have meaningful relationships, we need to trust each other, speak the truth and believe what others say, and respect others as individuals. These are the building blocks that will allow you to be effective in your cooperative and collaborative efforts. They, like all of the virtues that are developed over time, must be practiced with a dedicated effort. Let's begin our journey in this hall with the attribute of trustworthiness.

Trust

"Trust me." Those are influential words spoken from one person to another. The implied meaning is that you can rely on me. I have your back. I won't let you down. I will deliver. I will not weaken your faith in me. Trust is more than a word. When you ask another person to trust you, an invisible bond is established between the two of you that is sacred and unbreakable.

When we trust someone, a relationship is established between two or more people or entities. It involves truthfulness, honesty, and reliability. For trust to work, a person must be truthful. Lies only weaken relationships and erode any remnants of trust. Reliability is also a factor that is important. The more that we can depend on someone, the stronger the trust. When you trust someone, you are saying that you can count on the other person and they can count on you, no matter if either of you needs something or are in some kind of trouble. It is a bond of mutual and strictest confidence for each other's deepest thoughts and feelings. Trust and truthfulness are the foundation that helps us build friendships and relationships. Falsehoods and lies have the opposite effect.

Trust must be earned but it can also be easily destroyed. What if you lied to someone and they later found out that you lied? If that happened, people would have a difficult time trusting you. They would figure that if you lied once to them, you probably will do so again. Have you ever been betrayed by a lie? It hurts deeply when you learn the truth. Each lie is like putting a stake in your heart.

Another major obstacle to investing trust in someone else is when the other person decides to gossip and backbite. Gossiping is the act of spreading harmful rumors about a person or sharing information that the person was told in strict confidence. This may or may not be done intentionally to hurt, but the result is often the same. Backbiting, on the other hand, involves talking maliciously about someone to others. This act is intentional and designed to wound the other person out of meanness or to get back at them for something they did. Gossip and backbiting have a devastating effect on the spirit and can last for many, many years. They weaken trust and sow the seeds of mistrust and disunity.

Trust is a virtue that must be developed in any type of relationship. When people trust each other, they strengthen their positive feelings and develop deep loyalty. With friends, you can share your most intimate thoughts and they will keep your secret. Trust is essential in not only friendship, but with business partners, and in marriage. Distrust builds up walls between people, where trust tears down those walls. We learn it by trial and error. If you are to develop any type of relationship, trust is essential and vital in a world that is becoming more and more connected, and where the formation of relationships is needed to draw people closer together.

Truthfulness

TRUTHFULNESS IS THE BEDROCK ON WHICH ALL the other virtues are built. Being truthful is stating a fact, without distorting. How can you have a meaningful relationship if you don't tell the truth? As noted earlier, reliability, trustworthiness, and faithfulness are virtues with a close association to telling the truth. They are the cornerstone of friendships built over time. In contrast, lies, deceit, and manipulations distort the truth and are behaviors to avoid. Numerous lies damage relationships, even close ones, resulting in feelings of mistrust and betrayal. Make truthfulness a habit. As the old saying goes, "honesty is the best policy." You cannot have healthy interpersonal relations without it. While telling the truth to others is one thing, telling the truth to yourself may be just as important. Informed decision-making requires us to be honest, to be truthful, and aware of our thoughts and feelings.

How about telling a lie to avoid hurting someone's feelings? Is that ethical? Is it okay to lie in some situations? Is this the right thing to do? Sometimes we come across situations where there are no right or wrong answers, only gray. You have a difficult decision, but following your heart usually leads you in the right direction.

Engage in self-reflection at the end of each day. Take a personal inventory. Try to remember those you encountered today. Were you truthful, honest, or did you stretch the truth, or even lie? Was it the right thing to do or are you rationalizing? Tough questions.

Reverence

THERE ARE MANY FORMS OF REVERENCE, but it is most associated with our Creator and a deep appreciation and respect for all that is. Take your time, don't be in a rush, and enjoy the simple things. It is possible to experience reverence in nature and all forms of life. Such examples might be to spend your day off enjoying time at the local park, watching your little brothers and sisters playing, feeding the ducks, and maybe even fishing. Or, perhaps, hiking in the woods, enjoying the fresh air, the trees, the plants, and the wildlife. Sitting by a mountain stream, listening to the rush of the water, being mesmerized by its flow, you spend this special moment in reflection and meditation. Appreciation then results in your stand against climate change and taking measures to protect the environment.

What can you do to practice this virtue? Pray, meditate, and reflect on your own behavior. Take pleasure in life's positives—they are there if you look for them. Show respect for all living things and protect our world.

Honor

YOU PRACTICE HONOR WHEN YOU DEMONSTRATE respect for yourself and others. This is evident in the fourth commandment in the Bible to "honor thy father and mother." You give honor to your elders, but more important, you give honor and respect to yourself. You live by a code. No matter what everyone else is doing, you do what is right for you. You respect yourself and set a standard to live by. You do what is morally right and keep fellowship with the righteous. You are a role model for those around you.

Respect

CONSIDERATION FOR THE RIGHTS AND FEELINGS OF others, whether you realize it or not, is the beginning of respect. This formidable virtue creates a special connection between us and the people whom we honor like our elders or people of importance, and our friends and family. Respect is a feeling of admiration for someone because of who they are, their qualities, and the person that they have become. Courtesy is an extension of respect, where others are treated with the dignity they deserve.

Here are some examples of respect in action.
- **Respect is when we follow the directions of the teacher.**
- **Respect is when a minister is delivering a sermon to his congregation and**
- **everyone is listening.**
- **Respect is when we give sincere compliments to friends.**
- **Respect is when we help the elderly.**
- **Respect is given when we are before a judge and he/she is giving the verdict.**

Beyonce

Have you been to a Beyonce concert or seen her on film? She is absolutely amazing. Beyonce is generous, relatable, and a great role model for young girls. She emphasizes the importance of respect by accepting appearance, ethnicity, the LGBTQ community, and women in general.

During my years serving as a school psychologist and as a principal, it became apparent how important trust and respect between and among people are in social interactions. Respect requires continual repetition daily. You can't be respectful one day and indifferent the next if you expect it to be reciprocal. Like clockwork, it requires consistent, intentional effort. At Osawatomie State Hospital, in particular, respect was a necessary element between the staff and adolescents if there was to be any impact on the student's educational, social and psychiatric plans. The patients responded to care and concern, and in return, reflected the same feelings back in their own way, of course. Their records described heartbreaking backgrounds where abuse, distrust, and disrespect were a norm in their families. Most of them were treated as "sick" individuals, not good enough to live in society. That was the message they received outside of the hospital. With a little trust and respect, and the right medicines and training, amazing results could be seen with our clients.

There was one school in western Kansas where respect was the deciding factor. Many of my early experiences as a school psychologist were valuable lessons learned from grade school teachers. They were highly skilled after many years of teaching when it came to dealing with their students' education and well-being. On Monday mornings, the upper-grade teachers would set aside the first half-hour of the day to give the students an opportunity to talk about everything that happened over the weekend. It was a time for them to express their feelings instead of acting them out throughout the week. All families go through trials and hardships. The interactions at home, and sometimes not pleasant, had an effect on the children. The students let out their frustrations and feelings that originated over the weekend, allowing them to settle down and be ready for their work in the classroom.

To work, live, and get along with each other, respect is a necessary virtue. Listening to others, showing manners, being attentive so teachers can teach, working cooperatively with others, being prompt and finishing on time, showing kindness, and following an authority figure's demands are all examples of respect.

Visualization Exercise

Imagining going outdoors and discovering beautiful gardens with exotic plants, the sun shining brightly overhead and the birds singing in the trees. Straight ahead are the fountains of Sharing and Giving. The fountains are constantly circulating water for the pleasure of the viewers. The virtues that you will find here are helpfulness, compassion, sensitivity, courtesy, generosity, and kindness.

Helpfulness

THE MEDICAL STAFF OF DOCTORS, NURSES, AND health care workers is one group of professionals that comes to mind when thinking about the virtue of helpfulness. They are the heroes of this age where COVID and other diseases are afflicting our society. Risking their lives every day, they put in long hours and expose themselves to their own vulnerabilities, serving the sick and disabled. Policemen and firefighters are other examples of helping professionals who dedicate their services to the welfare of others. They are also considered heroes in times when crime and fires continue to rise. Teachers are the third example of an occupation that exists to serve others. Their mission is to help prepare students for academic excellence and citizenship. They demonstrate the very characteristics of helpfulness—assist, support, instruct.

Helpfulness is the act of providing service to people who are in need. Caring and concern for others provide the motivation to seek out people who require help. Look around. Find opportunities where you can assist those who require it. Just observe and be sensitive. Often, we need to be helped ourselves, even though we may not want to admit it. Don't be afraid to ask. Helpfulness stimulates cooperation and solidifies goodwill. How do you feel when someone is there to provide you with a helping hand? The response is usually thankful. And sometimes, it is a kind gesture just to let others help you. Being helpful is a blessing and contagious. Like all of the other virtues, it works best when you practice it daily.

Dr. Phil McGraw is a celebrity in the field of mental health, and can be seen on daytime television. His program, *Dr. Phil*, has aired over 2,000 hours during the past 13 years. He has taken on some tough societal issues—bullying, drug abuse, depression, violence, child abuse, and suicide, to name just some of them. His questions and his treatment are meant to help the guests and their families, and hopefully, guide them to seek further treatment. The national audience, along with the studio audience can then apply what they see to themselves or to people whom they care about.

Dr. Phil has been the recipient of 27 Emmy nominations. He is the author of seven #1 New York best sellers and has appeared nationally and internationally on news outlets, with people seeking his advice and expertise. He has been featured on *Today, Good Morning America, CBS This Morning,* and *Anderson Cooper*. His knowledge and helpfulness go beyond everything that has been mentioned. Dr. Phil's generosity is also noted. He started The Dr. Phil Foundation, which is a charitable organization that is non-profit and helps disadvantaged children and families. He has donated money to a variety of charities and uses his wealth to help others. This man is not only a role model for the average individual but for the famous and wealthy.

Helpfulness can have a snowball effect, not only making you feel good, but those around you, too. Open a door for someone. If someone is having difficulty with an assignment, offer your services. Fulfill your family duties, whatever they may be, such as cleaning your room, taking out the trash, or going to the grocery store. Each day, make a conscious effort to help those with whom you come into contact. Good feelings will be a natural result. Before long, it will become a habit.

Perhaps the best thing about helpfulness is that it not only raises your self-esteem, but empowers you to make a positive difference in this world. It is the best way to keep from dwelling upon negatives because it's impossible to feel sorry for yourself when you are focused on others.

Compassion

Compassion, simply stated, is a concern for the feelings of other people. When they are in pain or distress, you are there to listen and offer support. You try to identify with their feelings and their inner thoughts, lessening their isolation and aloneness. Having a well-developed reservoir of empathy is always beneficial when we encounter people who are stressed. Being there for them in times of trouble makes a monumental difference. Everyone needs support at one time or another. This message is solidified in the beginning lyrics of the Zac Brown Band song, "We're All in the Same Boat." Compassion connects us to each other and makes for a better world.

Angelina Jolie, an actress recognized around the world, is a fine example of the virtues of compassion, sensitivity, and understanding. Best known for her association with refugees, Angelina has contributed both her time and energy to lovingly support this group of children. She has traveled around the world visiting refugee camps and has been appointed Goodwill Ambassador to the United Nations High Commissioner for Refugees. Incredibly, Angelina has adopted refugee children from Cambodia, Ethiopia, and Vietnam. Her compassion for the suffering of these unfortunate children makes her an inspiration and role model.

The incredible Taylor Swift is also loved by millions but still remains humble and empathetic to her fans. She is ambitious and goal-driven in her career, but she has that innate ability to connect with her audiences and be a positive image for young people. On many occasions, her compassion for those in need is readily evident through her contributions and actions. According to Billboard, examples include: giving $15,500 to a teenage fan because her mother had spent the last three years in a coma, sending one of her fans a donation to help pay off her student loans, supporting her hometown library, contributing money to the African Parks Foundation of America after the release of her "Wildest Dreams" video, making a contribution to the Houston food bank after Hurricane Henry in 2017, giving $10,000 for a service dog after she meets a boy with autism, donating $10,000 to a fan battling cancer to help pay her medical bills, donating $1 million to the Nashville tornado relief efforts in 2020. and sending stimulus checks to her fans during the coronavirus crisis. Taylor has supported fans online who were being criticized or bullied. She takes the time to listen to others. Her empathy, kindness, and understanding have been factors in her success. Of course, her creativity and her innate ability to write lyrics and portray emotions in her singing, have also put her on top of the entertainment industry.

Story

Do you know the story about the mouse and the lion? The mouse bumped into a great lion and the lion was about to eat him when the mouse pleaded, "Please, don't eat me. Someday I will help you." The lion laughed at such an absurd idea, but let the mouse go anyway. Not long after, the mouse was strolling along and came upon the lion. The lion was caught in a large net and unable to free himself. The mouse remembered the time the lion spared his life and gnawed a hole in the net to free the lion. You never know when compassion will come back to you in a positive way.

Compassion is learned early in life. For most people, it is refined and developed over time but, like most virtues, it is never too late to acquire it. What can you do to practice this virtue?

When someone is upset, if you are uncomfortable talking, you can just sit there with them for support. Actions speak as loudly as words. Practice your skills in compassion with your friends. Try to understand if they are having trouble, maybe with another person, or if they don't have enough money to go to the Prom.

Sensitivity

Sensitivity is being aware of the feelings of others and a desire to help them cope with their pain and difficulties. It often precedes other virtues such as forgiveness, compassion, courtesy, kindness, helpfulness. You are aware of what people are going through and you want to be of service. You are attuned to their needs and care about their welfare.

Courtesy

Courtesy, as understood, is the consideration for others. Courtesy can also be recognized as a mild form of humility. You go out of your way to be polite to others. You try to make them feel good, to be recognized in a positive way through words and actions. Why practice this virtue? It makes people feel good. It makes people feel valued. It makes people feel special, and in turn, they will think the same of you.

Courtesy may be shown in such simple ways as saying "please" and "thank you." Other ways might be holding the door open for someone, waiting to be served last in line, letting a car merge in front of you in traffic, turning your cell phone off in a movie theatre, not interrupting a person who is talking, introducing people who don't know each other, and giving or passing along a compliment.

Courtesy is a very easy virtue to learn and practice. Sensitivity, another virtue, is a prerequisite. You just go out and do it by choosing to put other people before yourself.

Generosity

Generosity is the virtue of giving to others and not expecting anything in return. You might call it love in action. Generosity is a great way to show love and concern for others by giving them something that is meaningful or helpful to them. The act can involve a material possession, a service, or a part of your time and attention. When you partake in this process, you give not because you have to, but because it is in your heart that you want to give. Making people happy is the driving force. Giving anonymously, not expecting any recognition in return, is the highest form of generosity. Beware of bragging to others about your giving experiences. Instead of giving because you wanted to help others, it will appear that you just wanted praise and recognition for doing so, leaving you feeling empty and much less fulfilled.

We sometimes think of the rich as limited in this virtue. After all, they have millions or even billions. Even if they make charitable donations, they still have plenty of money so there is little sacrifice. Also, the contributions made by them are often shared publicly and they receive recognition for their actions. Certainly, there are rich people who give very generously without expectations of any recognition, but many times the poor, even when they give a small amount, offer a greater sacrifice to encompass the true nature of generosity.

There is a famous actor, in particular, who is known for his generosity and thoughtfulness. Can you guess who he is? He starred in the movies *Bill and Ted's Excellent Adventure*, *The Matrix* series, *Point Break*, *Speed*, and the *John Wick* series. Yes, Keanu Reeves is one busy person. Despite his fame and challenging schedule, he still finds time for those in need. He is one of the most generous stars in Hollywood. According to Patrick McLennan, a noted journalist and documentary maker, Keanu is one special person. For instance, his sister was tragically diagnosed with leukemia. Obviously in grief, he proceeded to give 70 percent of his earnings in *The Matrix* for leukemia research. That comes to approximately 24.5 million dollars. In order to help children worldwide, he established the Keanu Reeves Children Foundation, which has changed the lives of billions. He is also generous to his fellow co-workers. While filming John Wick 3, he gave each of the stuntmen a Harley-Davidson motorcycle for their hard work. He was presented with a contract for *The Matrix* sequels but changed it so that a substantial share of his profits went to the costume design and special effects team.

What a great way to demonstrate love by being generous.

The joy of giving sparks our spiritual souls, enriching lives, and spreading goodwill. Remember how you feel when someone gives you a gift or offers to help you in some way. It can be contagious, just like helpfulness. When you give to one person, if they are able, they often catch the spirit and pass it on. The giving keeps on going, forming a chain reaction. And, even if they can't do for another what you did for them, their elated spirit can affect others in a positive way.

Generosity in action can be seen when we give to others. We can contribute to charities, volunteer our time to assist the less fortunate, and participate in races for causes like breast cancer. There are many worthy charities one can choose from such as Wounded Warriors, The Salvation Army, and St. Jude's Hospital, and many others…the list is countless. For contributors, the mission is to select the charities you would like to support and follow through. Make generosity a habit, part of your daily routine.

Below are some helpful hints to make generosity habit forming.

- **Give money when you first get paid or receive your allowance. That way, you make sure to contribute.**
- **Look at your agenda. Free your calendar to make room for opportunities to serve the needy which, in turn, increases your understanding and compassion for their situation.**
- **Reach out to people in your community; don't limit your generosity to the people you love. Remember the words that Jesus spoke in the Bible: "It is more blessed to give than to receive."**

Kindness

Loving and caring, she won the hearts of the British people and the world. She had the extraordinary power of reaching out and touching the hearts of others. Her feelings were evident in the kindness and love she displayed in her many good works, setting her apart from her peers. People were devoted to her because she was devoted to them. No one questions that Princess Diana left her mark upon the world.

Even as a teenager, Princess Diana demonstrated a concern for the welfare of her friends. She later carried out this concern for others on a global scale as well. Diana walked the land mine fields in Angola in protest, reaching out to the victims. She was there for the lepers in Indonesia and for AIDS patients around the world. Her kindness and thoughtfulness earned her the love and respect of millions. Princess Diana spent her life assisting the sick and the poor. It was no surprise that a million people attended her funeral and captured a worldwide television audience.

Kindness originates in love. Sensitivity and compassion are the underlying tools. Everyone has enough love within themselves that they can reach out and share that love. This virtue is the true power of every human being—everyone has the ability in some way to make a positive difference for someone else. Words and deeds are the instruments we use to spread kindness—to make **all** people feel special and touch their souls. This virtue is generally taught early in life by our parents at home, at school through the teachers, and as young adults in the charitable works of churches and organizations. By adulthood, the foundation of this virtue should be established and well-planted within us. But whatever the age, kindness can be learned through awareness, focused attention, and a craving to give a part of yourself. Like other virtues, kindness is contagious with a ripple effect. People who pass it on affect the lives of others who, in turn, pass it on to even more people. Nobody truly knows the total effect it has on the world, only that it most certainly does.

Kindness can be practiced at any time or any place. Find someone and reach out to them. From the heart, be tender and considerate to discover their needs. Treat the stranger as if he were a loved one. And don't forget the animals. They need love and kindness too.

Visualization Exercise

Take a couple of deep breaths. Close your eyes. Do a short meditation. Open your eyes and return to our visualization. You are strolling through the garden and come upon a large building that houses statues involving hard work and dedication. You can tell that these virtues have to be practiced over time in order to take shape. These virtues include responsibility, reliability, perseverance, determination, self-discipline, tolerance, and patience.

Responsibility

Responsibilities are a part of life. As a baby, responsibilities are few. Parents, relatives, and siblings take care of all needs. Students in grade school have more duties such as brushing their teeth, taking a bath, combing their hair, getting dressed, and performing chores. There is work to complete in school and homework to do in the evenings. As we grow older, our responsibilities increase and we are faced with a whole new set of problems. One of the main differences from the earlier stages is the new realization that other people are now depending on *our* actions.

With responsibility comes accountability. People are depending on our actions as we depend on our own intellect and morals which are challenged with more complex duties. But in accepting that dependability, you take ownership for your actions—what you do and what you don't do. Excuses are held to a minimum. Instead, you admit to your mistakes and try to put forth your best effort.

You are responsible when...

- **You are on time.**
- **You are punctual.**
- **You respect the time of others.**
- **You make sure that people can rely on you.**

- **People don't have to tell you again and again what to do.**
- **You accept the consequences of your actions.**
- **You become successful because of your habits.**

You might remember the story of the *Three Little Kittens* from your childhood. Put simply, this poem reminds us that there are consequences, either positive or negative, for our actions.

Story

The three little kittens lost their mittens and they were punished for losing them, so their mother didn't give them any pie. In other words, they were irresponsible. Then, lo and behold, they found the lost mittens. Thus, they demonstrated responsibility. The mother, excited about the responsibility shown by the kittens, rewarded them with pie as a consequence.

Rewards, as in this story, are a result of positive choices, and punishment is often the result of negative choices. The great Winston Churchill took responsibility to a new level. He said that we are accountable even for the thoughts we think.

Become aware of your responsibilities and follow them to completion. Be dependable so people can rely on you. Do your part as a member of a team, whether it is at home, in the classroom, on the playing field, or at your job. If you are at school, your responsibility is to go to your classes, study, and pass your classes. On the playing field, you have to practice, do conditioning, learn the plays, and work in unison with the other team members. At home, you work with your parents to determine your duties. At your job, your boss will tell you what to do. The greater the number of responsibilities, the more you will accomplish, and the more important accountability becomes.

Reliability

If you say you are going to do something for someone, you do it, without being reminded.

People can count on you to get something done. You demonstrate dependability. It is important at home in doing chores and helping with responsibilities. It is important at school for classroom projects involving others, or playing your role in sports or the arts. It is very important in your job outside of school to show up on time and do your assigned duties. You keep your commitments.

Perseverance

To persevere means to not give up, no matter how difficult a task you are facing. When you face a difficult challenge, you will run into roadblocks to prevent your progress. No matter how hopeless, you must maintain the will to go on. There are two stories that come to mind when explaining the meaning of perseverance.

Story

A little train had a lot of cars to pull. The train did a tremendous job of pulling them until it came upon a steep hill. The little train tried with all its might, but couldn't pull the cars up and over the hill, so it went looking for help. The engine came across several big trains, but they wouldn't help. They had many excuses because they believed they were more important, more powerful, and of a higher quality. Why should they offer assistance to such a little and insignificant train? Finally, a little engine came along, approximately the same size. The little steam engine was willing to lend a helping hand even though it had never been over the mountain. The little steam engine tried to think positively, hitched itself to the train, and began to pull with all its might. As the little steam engine struggled up the steep mountain, you could hear it say over and over, "I think...I can! I think... I can! I think...I can!" Up they went. And yes, both of them made it to the top of the mountain and into the valley below.

Many of us need to follow the example of the little steam engine—persevere in difficulties, remain positive, and goal-directed. Following is another famous story from Aesop that you might recognize.

Story

Once there was a thirsty crow that came upon a pitcher. The crow noticed that there was some water in the pitcher, but it was too low and the neck too narrow for the crow to reach it. Somewhat discouraged, the crow attempted to knock the pitcher over, but found it to be too heavy. She couldn't move it. The crow became more determined and tried to push it, kick it, break it, but she failed in all of her attempts. After reflecting on the problem, the crow noticed that there were some small pebbles lying around and got an idea. She began picking up the pebbles and dropping them into the pitcher. Slowly, the water began to rise, and the crow was able to get a much-needed drink.

People with perseverance talk to themselves over and over. They silently say things like: "I know I can do this." "Keep on trying." "Maybe I need to solve this problem from a different angle." "If necessary, I will get help." Successful people remain positive and do not give up.

We know him as "The Rock." Dwayne Johnson, a household name in sports and Hollywood, was exposed to the gym as early as 5 years of age while growing up. He would watch his father, Rocky Johnson, and other professional wrestlers undergo an intensive training program whenever they were in town. He was allowed to begin lifting weights in his early teenage years. Because he learned what hard work was all about during his childhood years, he was persistent in his weightlifting regime, perhaps to the degree of obsession. He consistently pushed himself to the limit. Look where he ended up.

Life brings us many challenges as with this scenario: You are working on a car, trying to rebuild the engine. The task is more difficult than you thought. You Google information to guide you through the steps you are unfamiliar with, and you stay with it. You also get some help from one of your friends. Taking longer than you thought, you complete the task. Now is the time to take a drive and show it off to your friends.

Determination

Determination is similar to perseverance. Perseverance is the action *after* you set a goal or come up against a problem and put your full energy toward the completion or solution. Without it, things don't get done. In developing determination, you establish a habit, resistant to outside distractions, and stay on course.

Michael Phelps, a household name in the world of swimming, exemplifies the virtues of dedication and determination. At school, he was labeled with a diagnosis of attention deficit hyperactive disorder (ADHD), but luckily, he excelled in sports. A teacher at his school, which often happens to children with this disorder, told him he would never succeed in life. With desire and determination, Michael went on to prove this teacher wrong. As with any dedicated athlete, his training schedule was rigorous and time-consuming, beginning in grade school. By the time he reached high school, he would drive in the dark to the pool, then attended classes and continue his training afterwards. His life was committed to being the best that he could be. The training, in combination with his natural ability, propelled him into history. At the Olympics in Beijing, Michael won eight gold medals and set an Olympic record. He went on to set seven more world championship records. Michael Phelps had the drive and determination to become an American and World Champion.

A classic example of determination at work is also evident in the life of internationally known star Oprah Winfrey. Now, she is one brave soul who beat the odds to become one of the most successful and influential individuals of our time. Born into poverty in the segregated South, Oprah had to deal with many injustices that were endured by the African-American population during that time in history. She also had to cope with abuse in her preadolescent and adolescent years. Oprah had much to overcome at such a young age. Fortunately, she was extremely bright and possessed the gift of public speaking and conversing easily with others. She also had a clear idea of what she wanted in life, and the world would come to know her for her talents and determination. One of her most widely known accomplishments was the *Oprah Winfrey Show*, which ran for 25 seasons. On her show, Oprah dealt with a variety of topics, many of which were controversial. She used her own traumatic childhood to help others who suffered from similar ordeals.

As her fame grew, so did her generosity and countless donations. She always sought out ways to help others who were disadvantaged or struggling. In 2007, she established the Oprah Winfrey Leadership Academy for Girls in South Africa. In 2011, she started her own television network. Even though she was raised in an impoverished environment, Oprah Winfrey is now one of the richest and most charismatic individuals of our time. What a shining light that Oprah has brought to the world! She is a living example that determination can pay off if practiced.

When examining examples of both courage and determination, we can't leave out baseball legend Jackie Robinson. In a profession that was dominated by white athletes and jeering white prejudicial crowds, Jackie endured constant ridicule and hostility. He had to contend with unfair umpires, racial slurs, taunts, and unfair treatment on the field of play. He was often spiked while playing and hit intentionally by pitchers more times than any other player in the league. Despite all of this unjust treatment, his batting average was an impressive .311 over ten years and his speed and agility made him a terror on the paths to bases.

Determination is a virtue that everyone can achieve. Maybe not at the level of Michael Phelps, Oprah Winfrey, or Jackie Robinson, but it can have an impact on your life. This virtue requires you to focus all of your attention to achieve your chosen goal. Refuse to give up even though the task may be difficult, perhaps even thought impossible, until you are the master of it. Determination is a training ground where you develop habits to achieve personal goals. It only requires sustained effort and sacrifice, but it may not come without a price. For those who pay the price, success and good fortune may be awaiting them in the future.

Self-Discipline

According to the Oxford American Dictionary and Thesaurus, the definition of self-discipline is "the ability to control one's feelings and overcome one's weaknesses." When trying to make this virtue a part of your character, the first step is to set a goal. Then you can go about putting together efforts to achieve it. With careful thought, you can form actionable and measurable steps to guide you in achieving what you aim to accomplish. These steps direct the way for you. Take weight watchers, for example. A person usually sets a goal of how much weight they want to lose. Next, in trying to overcome their feelings and mental blocks toward food, their action step is to measure the amount of food they wish to eat. They weigh themselves weekly to determine their progress. Self-discipline must be exerted to reach the desired goal.

Athletes go through a similar process. Hours and hours of practice must be put forth every day to acquire the skills needed to perform on the playing field. Goals are set and reset in order to improve and be competitive in their sport. The want-to-be athletes may become angry, frustrated, and exhausted. Yet, they have to keep on working and sacrificing, maintaining control of their feelings, and constantly trying to build their strengths and manage their weaknesses. Whatever the sport—basketball, football, baseball, soccer, etc.—athletes must manage their feelings and improve their performance through self-discipline using effort and persistence.

Story

Most people remember the story of the tortoise and the hare. The hare was bragging about how fast he could run so the tortoise decided to challenge him to a race. The hare thought there was no way that the tortoise could beat him. The tortoise moved ever so slowly. A very confident hare, after seeing the slow pace of the tortoise, decided to take a nap. The tortoise, meanwhile, went at a slow and steady pace throughout the whole race. The tortoise passed the sleeping hare and eventually crossed the finish line, being declared the winner. The moral of the story is you may have more talent, but the person who works harder and puts forth more effort will eventually come out on top! Yes, self-discipline wins out in the end.

An important outcome of self-discipline is that you refuse to let your feelings dictate your actions. You use your mind and intellect to determine what is important for you to complete and develop. Once you know your goal, you set forth with action, and not words to complete it. Structure in your life is very important. Establish a schedule each day to fulfill responsibilities.

In your interpersonal encounters, use assertiveness when needed, not aggression. Demonstrate self-control rather than allowing your feelings to take over, especially in your interpersonal relationships.

Tolerance

Showing patience with the behavior of people who annoy you is tolerance in action. The more you dislike a person, thing, or event, the greater the need for tolerance since it becomes more difficult to practice. Let's say you have to go to a class. The teacher is boring! I mean really boring, but you have to go to pass. Each day you walk through the door, you know it is going to be bad, but you tolerate it. You demonstrate self-control, and you endure another hour.

You may not like to be around a person, especially because of their behavior or personality, but you put up with it without complaining or pouting. Oftentimes, you expect others to live up to your standards and beliefs, and when they don't, you can become irritated. But with great effort and tolerance, you overlook the faults and mistakes of others.

Patience

You have probably heard the phrase "patience is a virtue." Patience is a quality everyone would like to have but, like all of the other virtues, it requires practice. Remaining calm, while being reflective and tolerant when you encounter difficult and trying situations, is a good description of patience. When patient, you are willing to wait, put the needs of others first, and delay gratification for yourself. It doesn't necessarily have to be another person or persons. It might also be patience with extra work or in learning a new skill.

Scott Weaver clearly demonstrates what is meant by the word patience. Have you ever tried to make some object using nothing but toothpicks? According to *Be Amazed,* Scott is known for his toothpick sculptures. His most famous work is the re-creation of San Francisco called "Rolling Through the Bay." It stands nine feet tall and is comprised of 100,000 toothpicks. Thirty-five years is how long it took for him to complete the project. Famous landmarks, destinations, and attractions were included in this incredible art form.

Michelangelo, a 16th-century Italian artist, demonstrated patience when he painted the ceiling of the Sistine Chapel in Vatican City. The surface of the ceiling had curves, with an area of over 5,000 square feet. In order to complete the magnificent figures, Michelangelo had to tilt his head up for long hours. The project took him four years to complete. Thousands of people are drawn to this masterpiece every day, even though it was completed 500 years ago.

Patience is a beautiful and valuable virtue. It nurtures the soul and brings comfort to those around you. When bad news or trouble encompasses you, it is your patience that helps you weather the storm of tests and difficulties, providing you with strength and stability.

Story

The King and the Old Woman is a popular story on the value of patience. As the story goes, the King was in the forest on his way to a destination. Before he realized it, he was lost. One tree looked like another. He had no idea of how to escape. He tried to get to high ground, but still could not see any form of civilization. The night was beginning to set in, but in the distance, he saw a light in the darkness.

He came upon a house with an old woman living in it. Upon seeing the King, she offered him hospitality by giving him water to drink and a place to sleep. After his long journey, the King was also quite hungry, so the woman cooked a dish of rice and curry and served it to him.

The King displayed no manners whatsoever and immediately put his hand on the hot food. "Ouch!" he said, burning his fingers and spilling the bowl on the floor. Not knowing he was the King, the old woman said, "You are just like the King, way too impatient and impulsive. That is why you burned your hand and fingers when you tried to eat your food."

The king was surprised that the old woman would say such a thing. He believed he was neither impatient nor impulsive, so he asked her: "Why would you say that?" She replied in a very sweet and sincere voice, "Our king dreams of conquering and defeating all of his enemies' fortresses. Because of his impatience to defeat and eliminate all of his enemies at the same time, the end result will be great losses to his army. Instead, the king should focus his attention on the small forts, fortify them, and then move on to the larger forts.

Suddenly, the King understood. Why didn't I think of that? He needed to have more patience to avoid future problems. We can't always succeed when we just want quick results. In life, we sometimes have to think things through and take one step at a time.

Story

Remember the spider in the children's book "Charlotte's Web"? The spider could perform spectacular feats. She made Wilbur, the pig, famous. Spiders are often seen as creepy and many people are afraid of them, failing to see them as the incredible creatures that they are. Have you ever watched one spin its web? They begin by spinning a rather long thread. Next comes a second thread, which because of the even longer length, might break and result in the spider falling to the ground. If that happens, it will climb again and begin anew. It might make a second attempt and fall again, then a third attempt or maybe even more. It finally completes the web, but the task required a great amount of patience and concentration.

The next time you are around a person who has made a mistake, listen to him, using active listening. If you have to spend time with a person you don't like, tolerate him. If you do something stupid that the whole school becomes aware of, then deal with it and own it. In time, it will be forgotten or become less important. You aren't perfect and neither is anyone else. If you are having trouble waiting for the big concert this weekend, it will be here soon. Accept the delay in your gratification. With all these types of challenges, you're learning and practicing a major lesson in patience. Relax and take one day at a time.

Visualization Exercise

As we make our way out of the gallery, we have one more room to experience - the one of inspiration. On the paintings that cover these walls are the virtues of beauty, creativity, courage, forgiveness, and humility.

Beauty

Beauty brings you pleasure, joy, happiness. You experience it through all of your senses—sight (sunrise and sunsets, majestic mountains, flowers in a garden), hearing (the babbling of a brook, the singing of birds in the trees, the melody of songs in church), smell (a sweet-scented rose, the fragrance of perfume, a fresh baked pie), taste (ice cream on cake, ice tea, fresh home-made bread), touch (a silk sheet, the warmth of a campfire in autumn, cuddling with your loving pet). Beauty is what friendship and family are all about.

Creativity

Have you ever heard the saying that young kids are full of creativity, but as they progress through school, their creativity goes away? That may be true or not true, but the fact that creativity needs to be cultivated and reinforced is true. How many bright young people are in jobs that require none of their skills or talents and their creativity is wasting away? This virtue desperately needs to be fostered in our schools and wherever it can. The arts especially penetrate the spiritual core of children and youth to hold a special place.

Walt Disney was a genius when it came to imagination and creativity. The legacy that he built is known worldwide. His creations continue to entertain us and bring out the child within us. This entrepreneur's first creation appeared in the animated film *Steamboat Willie*. We know him as Mickey Mouse now. Later works included the *Three Little Pigs* and *Snow White*. Walt Disney, a source of abounding creativity, became an integral part of our culture with his cartoons, animated films, and two amusement parks—Disneyland and Disney World. He was awarded numerous Oscars in his lifetime and his empire has grown to be one of the largest media and entertainment centers in the world.

In the musical realm, Ray Charles was considered a genius. He played the piano, wrote songs from the heart, and was a dynamic singer. Ray wrote and sang music that spoke to the soul of the people, a sound totally his own in the 1950s. He combined blues, gospel, and jazz for a unique sound that resulted in much success for him. Ray created multiple hits and won Grammy Awards for his songs "Hit the Road Jack" and "Georgia on My Mind." He was also inducted into the Rock and Roll Hall of Fame. Remarkably, he was handicapped by blindness, but Ray Charles left a legacy of originality and a gift to future generations. He exercised his creativity.

To exercise this virtue, you could take a drawing class. How about photography? Maybe learning to play a musical instrument is the right choice for you. Creativity is not limited to just the arts. You can be creative when you write a poem, act in a play, cook a new dish, fix up your car, or rearrange the furniture in your room. Don't be afraid to try and explore—that's all part of the creative process. With each attempt, you create an opportunity to do something that is uniquely your own. Use your imagination and don't over-think. Creativity is within all of us.

Courage

Most people know when they acquire the virtue of courage. They attempt to deal with or confront some problem in their life. They may try something daring, something never tried before like bungee jumping, sky diving, windsurfing, or speaking in front of a large audience. Having courage is to be brave on the outside even though you might be experiencing feelings of fear and anxiety on the inside. Courage comes from attempting new things. You might be afraid of trying to overcome a problem, but you do it anyway, working through the fear. Any time you ask a person to change something in their personality and face problems of their past, it takes a courageous person to bring the problem to consciousness and then develop a plan to combat it. The courage to make changes in your life is never easy.

We all have had our own lessons with courage. Sometimes life throws problems at you that you are forced to deal with whether you like it or not. How you deal with these tests and difficulties determines how you go about developing your character. I was confronted with one of those life difficulties back in the spring of 1975.

A friend of mine and I decided to hitchhike from the college town of Hays, Kansas on our way to Kansas City. Back in the 1970s, it was considered safer to hitchhike than now. Our first ride took us as far as Salina, Kansas where the driver proceeded to let us out on the Interstate. Letting us out there was not where we wanted to be, but what were we to do? Before we had a chance to hitchhike further or get off of the Interstate, a police car pulled up and the officer picked us up, and took us straight to jail. The charge was *pedestrians on the Interstate*. A state of shock is what we were in.

There was no opportunity to make a phone call and there was nothing we could do or say to help ourselves. Since the incident occurred on Friday, we were put in jail until our court appearance which was on Monday. In jail, there were three cells that they called "tanks" which was where the prisoners were housed. We were thrown in tank one. What a sinking feeling I had when I heard the cell door clank shut and I eyeballed twelve other prisoners staring at us. It was so traumatic that the sound of the door closing plays out in my mind even to this day. The best way I could describe it was a sickening feeling. Fear, intense fear, consumed me, but that was just the beginning.

That night started out rough. The other prisoners did not like one particular jail-mate and they lit his bed on fire with him on it. *Oh no!* I thought. *What next?* I was terrified. There was no way out and we were going to have to handle whatever came our way. That is also the moment I learned my biggest lesson in courage. This take action virtue empowered me to come out of my shell and make friends with everyone in the tank. I did this by using my thinking skills and treating people with respect, despite what they did or who they were.

One inmate whom I met talked with me as if I were one of his friends. I later discovered that he had killed his son. Was this weekend ever going to end? Since I could play chess, this helped pass the time away. I was good, so most of my cell mates wanted to play chess with me. I played with everyone who wanted to play. After all, would you turn anyone down in that environment? One prisoner became angry when he was losing, so he overturned the table with the chess set and threatened me. Luckily, the other cell mates came to my rescue. Playing chess made me an "okay" guy because we found common ground where we were equals, and no one messed with me. At long last, it was Monday. We paid our fines and called our parents, and that was humiliating in itself.

Courage is what the children of St. Jude's Hospital show as the days, for them, turn into an eternity. Fighting for their lives, knowing that cancer is inside them and hoping for a miracle, these courageous children never give up. Parents and family, with their own fear and anxiety, stand by their children offering support and comfort, while staff work for a cure. Fear, pain, love, encouragement, disappointments are emotions that run rampant from one moment to the next. Cancer is a disease these children didn't ask for and certainly didn't deserve. Each day presents another series of obstacles, as they and their loved ones anxiously reach for hope. The hospital's mission is to advance cures and combat cancer growth in children of all races and creeds. The staff at hospitals such as St. Jude's create an environment of care and compassion in their treatment of children.

My son's best friend was one of those unfortunate individuals who was plagued with cancer. A growth was detected on his neck when he was a senior in high school. Immediately after hearing that it was cancerous, fear set in for him, his family, and those who loved him. He and his mother found their way to St. Jude's Hospital. The doctors, the nurses, and the staff were all that they advertise—professional, compassionate, loving, and competent. They gave hope when everything else was scary and uncertain. The pain, the struggle, and the ups and downs of treatment played a major impact on my son's friend and his mother who devotedly stood by his side in the hospital and throughout the treatment. Brave and courageous, they faced one day at a time. His mother posted faithfully every day on the *Caring Bridge* website to keep everyone informed of his progress. He had an extensive network of people following and supporting him. They believed their motto: "We Got This." Sometimes all you can do is pray, hope, love, and follow the expertise of the doctors. This young man faced his diagnosis and eventual death with courage. His soul is now soaring in the heavenly realms.

The virtue of courage can be found in all walks of life. In the military, brave men and women put their lives at risk to protect our freedom. Many of them die or suffer from life debilitating injuries that they have to endure for their entire life. Veterans have a special place in our society, deserving the utmost honor and respect. Their courage and the sacrifices they endure make them role models for our children and future generations to come.

Being afraid is okay in new and challenging situations. There will be times in your life when you have to stand up, even though you might be afraid, and face a person, problem, or situation. Develop your confidence. Try new things. Do not limit your world by being backed into a corner. When you take these small steps to be brave, courage will follow regardless of fear.

Forgiveness

When we reach the level of forgiveness, our anger becomes controlled, self-esteem goes up, and we reach a spiritual plane where it becomes possible to look beyond our needs and be of service to others. If anger, for whatever reason, continues to reside within us and has no release or outlet, forgiveness is blocked and it is impossible to bestow it on another.

West Nickel Mines Amish School

In 2006, Charles Carl Roberts IV took a classroom of Amish children captive. He bound and shot them before taking his own life. Five of the children died. That same day, the families of the children reached out and forgave Roberts. They went to the homes of his wife and parents to console them for their loss. They even attended the killer's funeral. It was the grandfather of one of the children shot who warned others from hating the killer. He said, "We must not think evil of this man" while another father said, "he had a mother and a wife and a soul. And now he's standing before a just God."

Story

Just the other day, I was watching a sitcom on my flat-screen TV. The mother's son discovered the woman of his dreams whom he wanted to marry. His mother was so excited and the day finally arrived when she was going to meet her. As the couple walked through the door, the mother was stunned. Her son's fiancée was of African-American descent. How could he do this? The mother's prejudice immediately blinded her eyes to her son and future daughter-in-law's love for each other. She couldn't accept this. She could never forgive her son.

The next day, the parents of the soon-to-be bride arrived for a much-anticipated visit. As they opened the door, they were mortified. How could their daughter marry a white man? There was much tension in the house. They could never forgive their daughter for such an ill-advised marriage. What poor judgment on the part of both of the children!

The next day arrived. Their children had to speak to all of them together. What could they possibly say to alleviate their parents' anger? They informed their parents that the girl was pregnant and that if they couldn't accept their marriage, they would move away. For the first time, the parents began to let their reasoning, not their emotions, react to the situation. If they persisted with their biased opposition, they would never experience the joy of watching their grandchild grow up; they would miss out on the love of their children.

They understood this would create a void in their lives and, for the first time, saw that their prejudice and pettiness were insignificant. They quickly forgave their children, but more importantly, they forgave themselves by acknowledging their prejudices so they could move on and be accepting. And their children forgave their parents for their prejudices because the parents recognized the need to change.

Forgiveness is a two-way street, benefiting both people simultaneously. When you forgive another and show mercy, you heal both them and yourself, strengthening a personal relationship and a spiritual connection. And even if the other person is reluctant to receive your forgiveness, do it for yourself. Self-damage occurs when you let resentment control your thoughts and feelings.

Forgiveness is the act of not harboring ill feelings toward a person, even though they have hurt you or someone you care about. Depending upon the severity of the hurt, this can be a challenging virtue to carry out. To consciously refrain from holding a grudge against a person, even though they harmed or offended you, is the essence of forgiveness. Someone may do you harm either accidentally or on purpose. When accidental, you can reason that they really didn't mean any harm. When it is on purpose, the challenge to forgive becomes greater because their intentions were deliberate. Their intentions were to hurt you or someone you love. In this case, detachment and self-control have to be exercised to manage your anger, thoughts, and feelings. But important to note is that forgiveness does not mean dismissing the wrong that was committed against you or the person you love. To forgive is a virtue, but to forget makes you vulnerable in the future.

Forgiving others is one thing, but forgiving yourself may be more difficult. Oftentimes, we dwell on our past mistakes, holding ourselves accountable and refusing to let go of them. Look in a mirror and make a pack with yourself to change and not make the same mistakes that were made in the past. Take positive actions and make a conscious effort to not dwell on the negative. Tormenting yourself over your wrong-doings will keep your energy depleted and reduce your productivity. Unwillingness to forgive is a major cause of unresolved anger in us. Make sure that your life is full of positive encounters, even with yourself, so that you can experience the joy of living.

Humility

This virtue requires a lot of practice and consistency. It has a lot of aspects, but you basically realize everyone is important, not just you. Giving service to others is natural and fulfilling. You don't think badly of yourself or others, but if you make a mistake, you own up to it and, with a sincere attitude, you seek to correct it. You have an appreciation for life and it shows.

There is one special individual who comes to mind and typifies humility, standing out as a role model. Mother Teresa, a Nobel Prize winner, dedicated her life to working with the poor, the sick, and the dying. Her works in India are unprecedented. Mother Teresa founded the Missionaries of Charity in 1950 which focused on "the poorest of the poor." Small in stature, this humble servant was a giant on the world stage. She worked diligently in a spirit of love and kindness, performing extraordinary work, and caring for anyone who needed help.

Pope Francis is a world-renowned leader who is also known for his humility. He is the leader of 1.2 billion Catholics. Pope Francis has simplified his personal living style, even more so than previous Popes. He drives a Ford Focus and lives in a two-room apartment. Pope Francis has urged people to look after the poor and he lives the life of what he advocates. He has been known to wash the feet of those considered outcasts from society, grants an audience with gay prisoners, and even, allegedly, slips out at night to feed the poor. His humility, compassion, and dedication to those in need, and to his followers, define and exemplify his mission in this world.

In the state of humility, recognizing that we are all equal to each other in value, you do not serve others for praise or recognition, but because they need help and are less fortunate. They might be sick, poor, orphaned children or elderly people. Your service to help others is its own reward and there is no need for praising or acknowledging your accomplishments.

Humility is also taking a look inwardly and developing a personal inventory. When you recognize your mistakes and weaknesses, and learn from them, that helps you become free of passing judgment on others for their mistakes or their misgivings—we are all fallible. Instead of being concerned with other's faults, you practice developing your own skills and gifts, with the goal of giving service in mind. There is no judging, no comparisons, just helping others before yourself. The golden rule comes into play: "Do unto others as you would want them to do unto you." In humility, you realize we are all empowered in this world to make it better, and we must do our part.

But, there is a threat to developing humility. It is always challenged when you acquire more power, prestige, and recognition for your accomplishments even when not sought.

The more successful you become, the more powerful you become, and the greater the probability that you could lose sight of where your source of power comes from. You might begin to think you are better than other people and you could let your ambitions get the best of you. You begin to let your humility slip away.

Develop self-control and be aware of humility. Set a goal each day to incorporate it into your mind, heart, and actions. Shake off the notion that you are better than others; this leads to pride. Comparing yourself to others could cause you to lose your confidence. Some people come by humility naturally. Others do not and they have to work harder. We all have different gifts and talents, and it is the responsibility of each of to use them wisely.

Applying Your Virtues Exercise

- You are a member of the United States soccer team and you are playing Iran to advance in the World Cup competition. In a nail-biter, your team wins by one goal. You see the Iranians bent over and lying on the ground, devastated. What is your reaction? What virtues, if any, do you demonstrate?
- You need to make a trip to the area thrift store. Outside, you notice a person with a sign: "Please help my family." She has two children with her. What is your reaction? What virtues, if any, would you demonstrate?
- You have been playing baseball since second grade. You have advanced skills by the time you reach high school. You are so good that a scout signs you to a contract with the ball club he represents, but assigns you to a minor league team. Your dream is to play in the major league. What is your reaction? What virtues, if any, would you demonstrate?
- You are taking an art class for the first time. Pottery turns out to be your favorite form of expression. You produce a number of clay items for display around school. What is your reaction? What virtues, if any,

would you demonstrate?
- You are driving along the road and you see a woman with a flat tire sitting in her car. What is your reaction? What virtues, if any, would you demonstrate?
- You are stopped at a light and you notice a man on the side of the road begging. You have seen him before and he seems to be a regular. What is your reaction? What virtues, if any, would you demonstrate?
- The house is in an uproar. Your sister has been in a car wreck. What is your reaction? What virtues, if any, would you demonstrate?
- Time to go to class. You hate it when you get paired up with Jeremy to complete an assignment. What is your reaction? What virtues, if any, would you demonstrate?
- You're in a hardware store. An old man is carrying some rather heavy items as he gets ready to leave. What is your reaction? What virtues, if any would you demonstrate?
- Your computer seems to be broken. You have spent hours working on it. What is your reaction? What virtues, if any, would you demonstrate?
- There is an alley behind your house which you often use to go downtown. A guy approaches and starts to make trouble for you. What is your reaction? What virtues, if any, would you demonstrate?
- There is a cat you noticed the other day near the gas station who looks underweight. What is your reaction? What virtues, if any, would you demonstrate?
- Time has passed slowly. You continue to wait at the dentist's office. It has already been 45 minutes since you arrived. What is your reaction? What virtues, if any, would you demonstrate?
- A friend wants you to lend him $50. He said he would pay you back next week. What is your reaction? What virtues, if any, would you demonstrate?
- It's Christmas Day and your family wants to attend

church together. What is your reaction? What virtues, if any, would you demonstrate?
- Your parents are getting a divorce. They tell you over the weekend. What is your reaction? What virtues, if any, would you demonstrate?
- The Big Brothers/Big Sisters Program is asking for volunteers. You have some extra time. What is your reaction? What virtues, if any, would you demonstrate?
- A member of your cross-country team, a friend of yours, is failing a class that he needs in order to graduate. What is your reaction? What virtues, if any, would you demonstrate?
- A friend confides in you with some personal information. What is your reaction? What virtues, if any, would you demonstrate?
- A tornado ravages your neighborhood. Some people lose everything they have. What is your reaction? What virtues, if any, would you demonstrate?
- You witness a crime. The problem is that the robber is a friend of yours. What is your reaction? What virtues, if any, would you demonstrate?
- You make a trip to the cemetery. What is your reaction? What virtues, if any, would you demonstrate?

Taking Stock Of Your Virtues

VIRTUES ARE BASICALLY THE CHARACTERISTICS THAT help us to cope with life's challenges. Virtues, their acquisition and improvement through daily practice is one of our primary tasks as we spend precious moments on earth. They define who we are in this life, empower us to make this world a better place, and prepare us for life ever after. Virtues are qualities that are spiritual in nature and connect us to others while giving us the characteristics to cope with the challenges in our lives.

Previously, definitions, explanations and examples have been used to illustrate a number of virtues. So how do we determine our success in acquiring and using them? Our focus now shifts to the 27 virtues noted and creating ways to measure our progress. A simple way to show that is to make a chart as shown below.

On a 1 to 5 point scale, rate yourself with how often and how sincerely you perform each virtue. Be honest in your estimation and don't judge yourself. You are just trying to discover how you can be of service to more people while improving your character, and to see your progress. Once you have completed this task, ask a friend or someone you trust who knows you very well, to rate your demonstration of each virtue from one to five, just as you did for yourself. Do not show them how you rated yourself until after they have completed the task. This exercise gives you a more objective idea of how often you practice certain virtues and provides a basis for future goal setting.

Assessing Virtues Exercise

- **Rarely observe = 1**
- **Observe occasionally = 2**
- **Adequate, but need to improve by observing once every 2 to 4 weeks = 3**
- **Common usage, once a week = 4**
- **It's a gift, seen daily = 5**

VIRTUE	SELF	FRIEND	RELATIVE
Justice			
Faith			
Hope			
Love			
Trust			
Truthfulness			
Reverence			
Honor			
Respect			
Helpfulness			
Compassion			
Sensitivity			
Courtesy			
Generosity			
Kindness			
Responsibility			
Reliability			
Perseverance			

Determination			
Self-Discipline			
Tolerance			
Patience			
Beauty			
Creativity			
Courage			
Forgiveness			
Humility			

Now that you have rated your performance with all the virtues and determined those that you strongly demonstrate, and those where you could definitely use more practice, you have a baseline from which to track your progress. Try using a daily journal to help determine your growth. For instance, you may want to improve courtesy. Begin by being polite to people. Use simple phrases like "please," "thank you," and "excuse me" with an attitude of respect and goodwill toward others. You may open doors for people, and assist the elderly and those in need. If in the car, you might overlook the mistakes of others on the road by not honking your horn or getting too close to another car that has just cut in front of you.

Another example might be generosity. You can be generous with both your time and money. Help out at the local food pantry. Get involved in community events like clothing drives for the needy, or volunteer to help out at the local animal shelter or summer recreational program. Spend quality time where it counts. You can also be generous with your money. You could increase weekly donations to your church or there are many charities and worthy causes that you can give to. Just look at your budget, and decide how much you are going to give and what cause you want to support. Take time to make it a conscious effort. Those who give are those who receive.

Try to set a specific plan to reach your goal once you look at your data:

In the next 30 days, what steps will I take to achieve the goal?

In the next 60 days, what steps will I take to achieve the goal?

In the next 90 days, what steps will I take to achieve the goal?

What blocks will I come up against?

If I need help, where will I go to get it?

Upon reflecting on your progress, use a simple journal to track your success with one or two goals at a time. Otherwise, it is easy to get frustrated and you don't want to be discouraged and give up. As you focus on each goal, maybe share it with a close friend to help you stay motivated. Use a calendar or your journal to record what you do on a particular day, and write down the deeds you demonstrated for the virtue you chose to improve. Review your progress, or lack thereof, at the end of each week or at the end of each month.

Another idea involves practicing all the virtues at the same time. This is the one I use. Begin by writing down each virtue on a notecard. Place them in a stack. Then, each day, look at your schedule and the events you plan to attend. Here is an example: Church is first on the schedule since it is Sunday. There will be a lunch prepared after the service when the congregation will get together. Next, I am going over to a relative's house for an afternoon of fun and games. My cousin Stan will be there, the one I don't like because he is so hard to get along with. The day will conclude with spending a quiet evening at home.

I need to pick three virtue cards that display what I wish to practice. The virtue card of reverence would be a good selection to start with since I will be attending church. Next is lunch. Helpfulness is a virtue that fits that situation. There will be many opportunities to help prepare and serve the meal, not to mention clean-up. Afterward, I will go to my cousins' house where Stan will be. Tolerance is definitely the virtue to use here. Now, I have reviewed my schedule and decided the three virtues I will practice. I will remove those cards I chose (reverence, helpfulness, and tolerance) and place them on a dresser, table, desk, or wherever is convenient, making sure they are visible to me as a reminder. In the evening, I will write down in my journal the deeds I performed to demonstrate each virtue to reinforce and strengthen my progress.

Chapter 6: Everyday Miracles

Learn To Embrace Change

Change can be a difficult process for the average person, depending on the severity of the change. The human being has spiritual powers. This we know. One only has to see our capacities for imagination, innovative and scientific inventions, performance in sports, artistic and musical expressions, and creations. We must listen to our hearts and be inspired by the Spirit of Faith. Miracles happen every day. That is why we have the spirit of Hope, the inward source that helps us continue to try. If we don't have hope, then hopelessness sets in. Hopelessness weakens the very essence of who we are which causes us to give up.

When we talk about character (hope, heart, and soul), we are able to go where miracles are made. These attributes help us handle the pain and difficulties of living. Everyone has hardships; no one is free of them. When we remain positive, we fill our minds with optimism and downplay the negativity. Here is the bottom line: There is a purpose for each one of us on this planet. There are no individuals who are hopeless or forever damaged. Each person can lead a happy and productive life. That may take on many different forms with more than 7 billion unique and varied individuals on the planet.

Miracles are bestowed upon those individuals who truly want to make changes in their lives. Mercy, forgiveness, compassion, and love are gifts to help us along the way. These qualities draw us closer to the spiritual part of our human nature.

Dedication, hard work, and patience are prerequisites. Don't ever let someone tell you that something is impossible for you to accomplish. Miracles do happen when prayer, a pure heart, faith, and hard work are combined for the right intention.

The Power of Prayer

REGARDLESS OF WHAT COUNTRY YOU COME FROM, most people grow up with the belief which involves the existence of some higher power. Christianity is the religion most prevalent in the Americas and throughout the world. Christians pray to God through Jesus. Islam ranks second to Christianity in the number of followers. They follow the words of the prophet Muhammad and pray to Allah. Hinduism is the third largest religion and is practiced extensively in India. Whatever your religious belief, prayer is essential for our well-being.

Praying has many forms. It can be used to give praise, ask for forgiveness, or ask for protection for yourself and your loved ones. It can be used to ask assistance for others—a sick person, someone we love, or even a person who has died and gone to the next realm. What do most people do in times of stress and crisis? They pray! When we find ourselves in a disaster, our health is in jeopardy, or someone we love is in danger, chills go through our bodies, our hearts sinks, and we become scared, frightened, and worried. It is at this moment we take time to pray for our safety or for someone else. History can attest that prayer can lead to miracles, even for the average person. When we talk about personal transformation or transforming the world, prayer is indisputably a top priority in achieving our lofty goals. Prayer, combined with action, make changes that seem like miracles. When people are making major changes in their lives, they need a boost to get them motivated and to have the fortitude to keep trying, never giving up. When alcoholics are trying to remove their addiction to alcohol, they require a spiritual connection along with hard work, as is the basis of Alcoholics Anonymous. Breaking a smoking habit is another difficult road to travel when a person becomes addicted to nicotine and struggles painfully to obtain freedom from the drug. The prison population may be the people needing the most help. Rehabilitation is critical as they are challenged to replace their destructive and antisocial behaviors with the reinforcement of social and spiritual principles. The goal is to teach them a trade and reinforce the importance of spiritual training, combined. Hope, usually through the spirit, is always available to us.

So What Is A Miracle?

When a special needs child with low self-esteem, who is engulfed with fear and inferiority in their very soul, receives special help, attention, and love, you witness the blossoming, radiating joy and happiness that every child deserves.

When a child is released from an orphanage and becomes a member of a family who loves and adores him.

When a mother gives birth and sees her child for the very first time. The whole family and friends celebrate.

When a person, who is addicted to drugs that rule him, breaks free of the addiction and returns to a life full of hope and direction.

When you find that special person to love, and both of you remain married until death.

When a person with a disabling injury or disease receives the right intervention, and remission occurs or the disease mysteriously disappears.

When the world learns that people are not just citizens of specific nations but citizens of the world, unity in diversity becomes the golden rule.

Chapter 7: The World Needs You!

We live in a world full of hardships, pain, and suffering. We have to undergo challenge after challenge as we journey through life. The traditional family unit is being challenged by divorces and separations. There are people starving in countries because of governments that can't get along with each other. Poverty continues to become more rampant as the gap between the wealthy and the poor widens. The rich are able to use their wealth to obtain special favors, sometimes avoiding justice. Climate change is causing catastrophes across the world—flooding, forest fires, drought.

Prejudices continue to plague our society. Radical groups and fanatical extremist religious sects are attacking cities and taking the lives of innocent people. Terrorist attacks continue to be on the increase. Racism is active, unveiling its destructive forces. Mass shootings are skyrocketing in our country, killing innocent people and terrorizing the average American. Certain countries threaten nuclear holocaust while others continue their quest for domination by invading sovereign countries, and seek to replace democracy with totalitarianism. As the world watches with pain and anguish, executions are being used as a means of control, mass graves are being dug for the dead, and bodies are lying on the streets. Justice is lacking in a world that is crying out for it.

We also live in a world full of faith, hope, and love. Internationally, as mentioned earlier, the United Nations and Red Cross were created to help administer to the womb of the masses. Churches, in this nation, have outreach programs to send missionaries to countries in need of assistance in the fields of nutrition, social consciousness, and economics.

Organizations within this country like wounded Warriors, Children's Mercy Hospital, the Shriners, Feeding America, and the Salvation Army support families who must combat the hardships of misfortunes and afflictions that affect them. Our forefathers and many today still believe in the gifts and talents that have been bestowed upon us as a nation by the All-Knowing, All-Glorious, Compassionate Creator. Life is a miracle with artists, scientists, doctors, nurses, writers, singers, actors, Caucasians, African-Americans, Native Americans, and Asians— all living in the same country, same world, with different perceptions, viewpoints, and beliefs. Citizens from other countries and continents, downward to South America, across the ocean to Europe's war-torn Ukraine, Russia, China, North Korea, and across the waters to Australia also have the same gifts, talents, and different perceptions bestowed upon them. That is the beauty in the world we live in—the quest for unity amidst a world of diversity.

Individually, now this is where the story changes. Each of us was given our own life, unique from everyone else. Positive energy, flowing into the world, is generated by each person who strives to discover and become the person they were meant to be. Learn to celebrate your own life and not try to live the life of another. Do not compare your abilities and fortunes to others. This only leads us down the road of discontentment and unhappiness. Despite what is happening in the world, we each have our own emotions, both happy and sad; achievements and failures; joy and depression. This is the source of faith, hope, and love. It is never too late to make changes in your life.

Summary: Don't Give up. Celebrate Your Victories

Congratulations! You now have learned various strategies to help you manage anger and other unpleasant feelings. You know how to apply that knowledge and evaluate personal growth strategies to explore your inner-self, and you can use this book as a reference anytime. The illustrations that are included to assist you in understanding the materials and applying the information presented should come to mind when needed, and help you deal with stressful situations using the process of visualization. The strategies presented, involving your emotional and intellectual capacities, will provide you with confidence as you make your way through problem-solving situations.

Remember that anger and other painful feelings are normal, and that everyone, at one time or other, has problems channeling their anger. That is okay. We are human beings. The important thing is to first be aware of your anger and uncomfortable feelings, and then identify any that may be underlying so that you can manage them. You can also determine whether you should express them at the time or delay your reaction. If it is a major problem, take the time to think and meditate on it before you respond so you can make better decisions. If it is a minor problem, deal with it as the situation unfolds. As discussed in the book, if you aren't aware of your true feelings, they may become blocked, leading to physical problems like headaches, heart problems, high blood pressure, depression, and other undesirable afflictions.

Remember the importance of the virtues Faith, Hope and Love. Faithfulness instills the positive incentive to carry out plans, knowing that attainment will be inevitable. Hope eradicates feelings of loss and despair. Optimism is the result. Love is the unifying virtue. It is the reason for our existence—to love and care for each other. Your virtues are instrumental and endless in building your character, in becoming who you want to be. They allow you to serve others for the betterment of the world and give you the power to make that change. Spiritual powers also evolve, preparing you for the next stage of existence.

Remember to be patient—transformation does not happen overnight but is a process of hard work, dedication, time, and moderation that you incorporate into your everyday life. It requires you to take negative thinking and self-doubts, and convert them into positive productive thoughts. It involves identifying your feelings for effective problem-solving and self-reflecting on your moral and spiritual nature to improve your relationships, using your skills and resources to help others.

Remember to work with others, love others, and live life to its fullest. Be patient, work out a coordinated plan and work for improvement in your goals and aspirations. Focus on the positive. Everyone counts because everyone has a soul that was sent by the highest realm. When we get in touch with our spirit—the essence of who we are—miracles can and do happen.

Remember life is an ever-changing journey with lots of opportunity for personal transformation to make it what you want it to be. Don't be afraid to look at yourself and change what needs to be changed. Remember change is just a process incorporating hard work, dedication, and moderation using the three powerful virtues of faith, hope, and love. But, change is what we must *want* to do, that we feel we need to do; it can't be something that others want us to do. So let your virtues define who you are and what you can become. Make your life in this world count and live up to your potential—the world needs **you**. You are capable of amazing things. Strive for a life that honors yourself and those you love. Be kind. Work hard. Stay humble. Give assistance to others. Have faith. Never give up. Stay focused. Fulfill your destiny. **Be happy being you.**

Appendix A

Feelings and Rating Their Intensity, from Anchors and Scenarios, page 105.

When I'm backed into a corner	When I feel people are out to get me	When people make fun of me
1-Hassled	1-Uncertain	1-Embarrassed
2-Pressured	2-Cautious	2-Foolish
3-Controlled	3-Suspicious	3-Stupid
4-Threatened	4-Defensive	4-Degraded
5-Trapped	5-Guarded	5-Humiliated

When I don't know what I'm doing	Nobody loves me	When you let me down
1-Scattered	1-Lonely	1-Disappointed
2- Disorganized	2-Left Out	2-Frustrated
3-Puzzled	3-Rejected	3-Ignored
4-Confused	4-Deserted	4-Unimportant
5-Lost	5-Abandoned	5-Crushed

When nothing is going my way	When trust is broken	When worry is inside you
1-Sad	1-Offended	1-Tense
2-Empty	2-Deceived	2-Nervous
3-Depressed	3-Used	3-Anxious
4-Dejected	4-Hurt	4-Frantic
5-Defeated	5-Betrayed	5-Hysterical

When I just can't win	When I don't know what is about to happen
1-Insecure	1-Apprehensive
2-Lost	2-Scared
3-Helpless	3-Frightened
4-Hopeless	4-Terrified
5-Despair	5-Petrified

When things are going my way	When I show respect to others	When I'm doing things I like
5-Elated	5-Loving	5-Enthusiastic
4-Overjoyed	4-Affectionate	4-Energetic
3-Excited	3-Caring	3-Determined
2-Happy	2-Considerate	2-Involved
1-Good	1-Kind	1-Willing

When I'm praised	When it is all right to give my opinion
5-Valuable	5-Secure
4-Honored	4-Safe
3-Important	3-Confident
2-Wanted	2-Content
1-Good	1-Okay

Appendix B

Definitions/Categories, from Feelings How to Identify, page 92:

When I'm backed into a corner, I feel...
1 Hassled—someone won't leave you alone
2 Pressured—requires immediate attention
3 Controlled—you feel like a puppet
4 Threatened—to feel that someone is out to get you
5 Trapped—with no way out

When I feel people are out to get me, I feel...
1 Uncertain—not feeling sure about things
2 Cautious—watching for warning signs
3 Suspicious—problems relying on others
4 Defensive—leaning toward guarded
5 Guarded—high alert; self-preservation

When people make fun of me, I feel...
1 Embarrassed—makes someone uneasy in front of others
2 Foolish—feeling uncomfortable, like you did the wrong thing
3 Stupid—put yourself down, not capable of rational thought
4 Degraded—beating yourself up, feeling no good
5 Humiliated—downgrade a person in public

When I don't know what I'm doing, I feel...
1 Scattered—problems with focusing on one's thoughts
2 Disorganized—not organized
3 Puzzled—unable to make sense
4 Confused—have no idea of what is going on
5 Lost—feeling there is no way out

Nobody loves me and I feel...
1 Lonely—lack contact with others
2 Left Out—feeling hurt because you are not included
3 Rejected—tell a person no; totally ignore
4 Deserted—left all by yourself, causing an empty feeling
5 Abandoned—others run out and do not come back

When you let me down, I feel...
1 Disappointed—your expectation does not happen
2 Frustrated—hinders you from getting what you want
3 Ignored—do not give any attention on purpose
4 Unimportant—overlooked because you don't matter
5 Crushed—overwhelmed

When nothing goes my way, I feel,,,
1 Sad—not feeling good
2 Empty—feeling hollow inside
3 Depressed—so low that you feel unmotivated
4 Dejected—take it personally, hard to go on
5 Defeated—fail to succeed; feel like a failure

When trust is broken, I feel...
1 Offended—disregards one's feelings
2 Deceived—trick someone to take advantage of
3 Used—someone gets what they want at your expense
4 Hurt—pain from a person or event
5 Betrayed—to be a traitor, trust is impossible

When worry is inside me, I feel...
1 Tense—feeling uptight, not relaxed
2 Nervous—get all worked up, trouble controlling oneself
3 Anxious—agitation takes over inside you
4 Frantic—in a state of desperation
5 Hysterical—beyond control, overwhelmed

When I just can't win, I feel...
1 Insecure—lacks confidence in oneself
2 Helpless—can't stand up for oneself
3 Lost—totally on the wrong track
4 Hopeless—hope is nowhere to be found
5 Despair—hopelessness at its lowest

When I don't know what is about to happen, I feel...
1 Apprehensive—upset about future events
2 Scared—strike fear into
3 Frightened—a sudden intense feeling of fear
4 Terrified—striking terror in your heart
5 Petrified—stunned with fear, scared beyond belief

When things are going my way, I feel...
1 Good—experiencing a pleasant feeling
2 Happy—enjoying oneself
3 Excited—surge of positive energy
4 Overjoyed—great joy; feel like your floating
5 Elated—spirits are at their highest

When I show respect to others, I feel...
1 Kind—friendly; generous
2 Considerate—attend to the needs of others
3 Caring—showing concern for others
4 Affectionate—soft, warm, soothing
5 Loving—the greatest feeling of all

When I'm doing things I like, I feel...
1 Willing—agreeable; do it because it is your choice
2 Involved—give your full attention; caught up in
3 Determined—focus all your attention on something
4 Energetic—dynamic, bursting with energy
5 Enthusiastic—having great enjoyment, very excitable

When I'm praised, I feel...
1 Good—feeling okay, all right
2 Wanted—people want you around
3 Important—having great significance; mean a great deal
4 Honored—held to a higher standard
5 Valuable—worth a great deal; highly prized

When it is all right to give my opinion, I feel...
1 Okay—things are going all right
2 Content—feeling pretty good
3 Confident—being sure in one's abilities
4 Safe—free from the doubts of others
5 Secure—free from fear, care, doubt and anxiety

Appendix C

Evaluating your behavior, from Processing for Success, page 62:

To illustrate how the Processing For Success exercise works, two examples are listed below that were conducted with two teenagers.

Processing for Success—Evaluating Your Behavior

16-year-old male

1. **Date happened:** *a couple of months ago*

2. **Where were you when you became angry?**
   The little theatre at school

3. **What happened?** *I found out that one of my friends was talking about me behind my back. Then she said something to me with attitude.*

4. **Repeat:** "I am responsible for My Anger and My Feelings."

5. **What feelings came before the anger?**

- Controlled (3)
- Guarded (5)
- Stupid (3)
- Lonely (1)
- Crushed (5)
- Depressed (3)
- Used (3)
- Apprehensive (1)

6. **Did my feelings fit the situation?** *Yes*

7. **What did you do?** *Prioritize techniques using 1, 2, and 3.*

<u>1</u> breathed deeply	___counted backward
___Yelled	___talked to an adult
___thought ahead	<u>3</u> talked to a friend
___used profanity	___wrote a letter
___broke something	___positive self-talk
___visualized	<u>2</u> took a time out
___backbiting	___was threatened
<u>4</u> be assertive	___other

I had to get away so I took a time out. I did some deep breathing and told myself to calm down. I kept saying to myself, "I'm so stupid." I went and talked to a few of my friends to help me sort things out. I went back to my friend and I confronted her. I told her my feelings. I was assertive.

8. **What self-talk did you use?** *I told myself that I was stupid. Also, stay calm.*

9. **How did the other person feel?**

- **Threatened (4)**
- **Defensive (4)**
- **Foolish (2)**
- **Rejected (3)**
- **Ignored (3)**
- **Defeated (5)**
- **Used (3)**
- **Insecure (1)**
- **Anxious (3)**

10. What was the outcome?

I calmly confronted her. I tried to understand her point of view and her feelings. I stated my point of view and my feelings. She apologized and we resumed our friendship.

11. How angry were you?   *Furious*

**12. How did you handle the situation?   Good*

13. What is your plan for success in the future?

I will confront her sooner and don't overthink. I need to remain calm, do some deep breathing, and stop telling myself that I am stupid. I am not stupid. I can resolve this. I'll tell myself everything is going to be okay and deal with it.

Comments after the exercise:

I kind of knew how I felt, but not anywhere near the feelings I identified in this exercise.

I had no idea of any of her feelings.

I can see the situation more clearly now and will know what to do in the future.

This is really good.

Processing for Success—Evaluating Your Behavior
18-year-old-male

1. Date happened: *two months ago*

2. Where were you when you became angry?
football stadium

3. *What happened? I was walking out of the stadium. I was already upset because we were losing. Two guys were sitting on a table and they mumbled an insult using profanity at me. I stopped and said excuse me. They continued to use profanity and insult me. I didn't even know who they were. I said to come meet me in the parking lot. They followed me there but said they were not really into this.*

4. Repeat: "I Am Responsible for My Anger and My Feelings."

5. What feelings came before the anger?
- threatened (4)
- defensive (4)
- degraded (4)
- tense (1)
- frightened (3)

6. Did your feelings fit the situation: *I think so.*

7. What did you do? Prioritize techniques using 1, 2, 3:

_3_ breathed deeply	___ counted backward
___ Yelled	___ talked to an adult
___ thought ahead	_4_ talked to a friend
_2_ used profanity	___ wrote a letter
___ broke something	___ positive self-talk
___ visualized	___ took a time out
___ backbiting	_1_ was threatened
___ be assertive	___ other

8. What self-talk did you use? *What am I doing to get into this?*

9. How did the other person feel?

- threatened (4)
- guarded (5)   had a girl with them
- anxious (3)
- apprehensive (1)

10. What was the outcome? *My adrenalin was high. I'm glad I stood up for myself. The other guy backed down.*

11. How angry were you? *Enraged*

12. How did you handle the situation? *Poorly*

13. What is your plan for success next time?
Next time I think I'll do some deep breathing and just keep on walking. I'll just ignore them as if they weren't really there.

Acknowledgements

To my talented and dedicated editor, Vicki Julian, who made this book the best it could be. To my artist, Julia Cubiz, whose awe-inspiring illustrations captured the emotions and concepts presented in this book. And to my publisher, Maureen (Micki) Carroll, who gave me the opportunity to proceed forward.

About the Author

Dennis M. Hargis is an educator and psychologist with more than 40 years of professional experience working with children, adolescents and youth. He holds a Bachelor's Degree in Psychology, a Master's Degree in School Psychology, and a Certification in Educational Administration. While serving at Osawatomie State Hospital as acting principal for the school located on campus, psychologist and behavior intervention specialist, he provided direct services in educational programming, anger management, individual counseling, and crisis intervention. He also assisted with group therapy and biofeedback groups. As a staff member at the hospital, he participated in numerous, accredited training sessions with special emphasis ranging from psychiatric disorders to focusing on disturbed adolescents. He has also conducted more than fifty workshops, seminars, and presentations to share his program of successful methods in teaching anger management and problem-solving skills to adolescents

Additionally, Hargis has 17 years of working as a building administrator, both at a special purpose school and as an elementary principal in public education. In addition to his administrative duties while at LaCygne Elementary in Kansas, he served as the District Coordinator for the English as a Second Language curriculum, established the school's Foster Grandparent Program, and was chairperson of the school's multi-tiered support system and the student assistance team. As the creator of a unique and successful program, using identification of feelings and visualization to teach anger management and problem-solving skills to adolescents, Hargis uses his vast and varied knowledge to help young people be happy being themselves.

Hargis was raised in a loving home with a devoted love of God and the need to provide a lifetime of service to others. He now practices the Baha'i faith, which is a recent Global religion and was founded by Baha'u'llah. This religion is second only to Christianity in the number of geographical locations in the world.

About the Artist

Outcasted Art has been in business since 2016. Spray paint art developed into custom guitars, portraits, murals and now book Illustration and logo design. Julia Cubiz is a multi-medium artist who built her artistry business to give others a voice, transforming her clients thoughts, desires and passions into a visual work of art. Thanks to all the amazing clients that put their faith in Outcasted Art, Julia and her family of four are able to live a comfortable debt-free life. Julia battled with the thought of pursuing a career that put her in a leadership role for she was a very shy kid and dare I say, quite the outcast.

www.ingramcontent.com/pod-product-compliance
Lightning Source LLC
Chambersburg PA
CBHW050248010526
44107CB00003B/238